PRACTICAL GOLF

PRAC

TICAL GOLF

By **JOHN JACOBS**
with KEN BOWDEN

Illustrated by
ANTHONY RAVIELLI

Foreword by
TONY JACKLIN

Quadrangle/The New York Times Book Co.

Acknowledgments

Since the magazine was first published in March, 1962, I have contributed at least one article a month to "Golf World," Britain's biggest-selling golf periodical. Some of the material in this book first appeared in those articles, and I am most grateful to "Golf World" and its proprietor, The New York Times, for permitting me to abstract freely from them.

My co-author on this book, Ken Bowden, collaborated with me in writing most of the material taken from articles in "Golf World," which he edited for its first six years. I would like to thank him for his enthusiastic and patient help in that original creative process; for his efforts in helping me write much new material for this book; and for his collation and editing of the work.

My sincerest thanks also go to Anthony Ravielli for his wonderful illustrations. Ever since I first saw his work with Ben Hogan in "The Modern Fundamentals of Golf," Tony Ravielli has been, for me, the supreme illustrator of golf technique. I am honored that we should have been able to work together.

JOHN JACOBS

Library of Congress Catalog Card Number: 76-189149

International Standard Book Number: 0-8129-0274-2 (hardback) 0-8129-6268-0 (paperback)

FOREWORD

In 1963 I won my first money in a major British tournament by finishing 34th in the Coxmoor event. I took home nine pounds ten shillings. ($24), and I'll never forget the thrill of that first big-league check. But the tournament sticks in my memory for another reason — it was the first time I saw John Jacobs.

John finished second in that event. He was a star player in those days and I watched him, as I watched all the good ones, on the practice ground. He had an impressive swing, very firm and compact for so big a man — very much the sort of swing you see on the U.S. tour today. But what I admired most about his swing was his tempo; he is one of the golfers I sometimes still picture in my mind's eye when my tempo — the all-important factor in my game today — goes sour.

In the next two years, submitting to the demands upon him from many British and European sources as a teacher, John virtually hung up his clubs. But whenever our paths met he was one of those who gave me unstinted encouragement and help. In 1967 John had spent an hour with me on the practice ground before the final round of the first major tournament I won in Britain. At the 1971 British Open I sought him out for a late-evening session after the third round. In minutes he had me hitting the ball exactly the way I wanted to, and it wasn't his fault that I couldn't make myself do it on the golf course next day — at least, not until it had become too late.

Like most successful people in British sport, Jacobs has sometimes been the target of jealousy. But I believe he has done a lot more than just help a lot of individuals to play better golf. I think his influence as a teacher has been one of the factors behind Britain's new and growing impact on the international golf scene.

John's approach to hitting a golf ball is very much my approach — simple and direct, with great emphasis on "cause and effect." As I know from my own experience, putting golf technique down effectively on paper is extremely difficult. I think Jacobs does it superbly. This book is a wonderful distillation of an exceptional man's knowledge, and I don't see how it can fail to help any golfer to play better.

TONY JACKLIN

THE
AUTHOR

John Jacobs is a "born teacher," in the way that some people are said to be "born" athletes, or musicians, or politicians. Whatever he might have done in life he would have been good at himself, but probably even better at showing other people how to do it. He has the temperament, the authority, the knack, the vocabulary, and — although after an exhausting day on a driving range or practice ground he will deny it — the *desire* to teach. He gets deep pleasure and fulfillment out of helping people to master the extraordinarily difficult game of golf. Today his lesson fees are either a lot or nothing at all, and he is driven to go on teaching, I think, out of a sense of vocation. He is the type of man whose conscience would grow troublesome if he let his natural talent lie idle.

It could be that Jacobs knows more about what it takes to hit a golf ball than anyone in the world. Certainly no one in Europe is his peer. He started to learn golf at about the age of three at Lindrick Golf Club in Yorkshire, where he was born. As a boy and young man he wanted to be a better player than his natural temperament allowed, which launched him into an ever-deepening study of technique. His efforts then were stimulated by his own tournament ambitions, but, like most British professionals of that era, he taught at his club between events. Ultimately he became a victim of his own reputation, manacled to an appointment book and forced to forget his own playing aspirations to foster other people's. In an effort to reduce his teaching, to find time to practice, he once doubled his fees. The effect was simply to double the demand for his services.

In 1964 Jacobs accepted fate. He became chief executive of, and the driving force behind, Britain's major golf coaching and practice centers; and, through this and seemingly a few hundred other activities, established himself not only as the leading authority on how to play golf, but as one of its best-known personalities.

Jacobs is 51, a big, handsome man with a strong and restless personality, a direct manner, and, at times, a finger-wagging distinctly professorial air. He had considerable success as a tournament player, and would have had more if he could have putted as well as he handled the long shots. In 1955 he played for Britain in the Ryder Cup Match against America at Palm Springs, won his foursome match with Johnny Fallon, and went on to beat Cary Middlecoff — then a U.S. superstar — with rounds of 69 and 65.

Jacobs has taught the top amateur golfers of England,

Scotland, Wales, Ireland, Spain, Italy and France, and was official coach to the victorious British Walker Cup team in 1971. Today he feels he can get his message to more people — and personally gets most fun — by teaching young professionals how and what to teach (he takes great pride in their prowess). He has made three series of instructional golf films (two for TV), has published three books, and contributes regularly to newspapers and golf magazines throughout Europe and. America. He makes a high income from the game, but doesn't feel guilty about it because "I work twice as hard as most people."

I have worked closely with Jacobs since, as its editor, I invited him to become a founder contributor to the British magazine "Golf World" in 1962. During the decade of our association I have also come to know fairly intimately the top players and teachers of golf in most of the leading golf nations, especially the stars of the U.S.A. through my work in editorial positions at "Golf Digest" magazine. John Jacobs remains, to me, the most knowledgeable individual on golf technique I have ever met, and the finest practical teacher of the game.

Jacobs is an ambitious man, in the sense of wanting to use his talents to the full. But he sees his growing power and influence in golf as increasing his opportunities to serve it as well as fulfilling his personal aims. There is probably nothing in the game that he would take on without utter conviction that he could make a complete success of it. Above all, he believes that if he were in sole charge of coaching, Britain one day would be the best golfing nation on earth.

He is probably right.

KEN BOWDEN

CONTENTS

1.STRIKING THE BALL

2.PLAYING THE GAME

3.MORE PRACTICAL GOLF

1
STRIKING THE BALL

INTRODUCTION

First, understand what you are trying to do

"The only purpose of the golf swing is to move the club through the ball square to the target at maximum speed. How this is done is of no significance at all, so long as the method employed enables it to be done repetitively."

That is my number one credo. It is the basis on which I teach golf. It may sound elementary, but I am certain that the point it makes has been missed by most golfers. Ninety-five per cent of the people who come to me for lessons don't really know what they are trying to do when they swing a golf club. Their prime concern is to get into certain "positions" during the swing. Therein, they believe, lies the elusive "secret" of golf. They have either never known or have long forgotten that the only reason such positions are necessary is *to get the club to swing correctly through the ball.*

There are four possible impact variations produced by the golf swing that, in concert, determine the behavior of the ball. They are:

1. The direction in which the clubface looks.
2. The direction of the swing.
3. The angle of the club's approach to the ball.
4. The speed of the club.

Of these four, the alignment of the clubface at impact is the most vital. If it is not reasonably correct, it will cause errors in the other three areas. For example, the clubface being open — pointing right of target — invariably leads at impact to an out-to-in swing path through the ball. This in turn forces the club into too steep an angle of approach to the ball. The clubface *cannot* meet the ball either squarely or solidly. Conversely, a closed clubface at impact generally leads to an in-to-out swing path. That causes too shallow an angle of approach — the club reaches the bottom of its arc before it reaches the ball. Again, the clubface *cannot* meet the ball either solidly or square.

Do one thing right in the golf swing and it will lead to another right. Do one thing wrong and it will produce another wrong. In this sense, golf is a *reaction* game. Never forget that fact.

Most of what you read about curing slicing tells you to do things like "slide the hips as the first movement of the downswing," "stay inside," "tuck the right elbow in," "hit late," "hold back your shoulders," and so on, ad nauseum. Unless you cure the *basic* fault — your open clubface at impact—you'll never do those things. You *can't,* because your *natural reactions* oppose them. That is

15

Golf's four vital impact elements

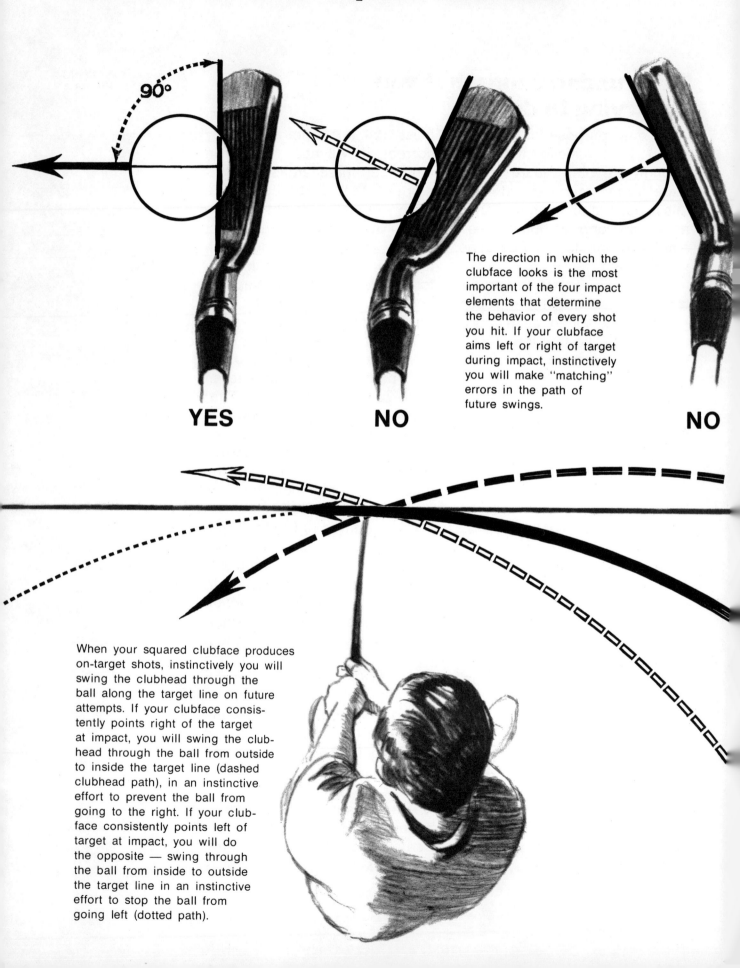

90°

YES   **NO**   **NO**

The direction in which the clubface looks is the most important of the four impact elements that determine the behavior of every shot you hit. If your clubface aims left or right of target during impact, instinctively you will make "matching" errors in the path of future swings.

When your squared clubface produces on-target shots, instinctively you will swing the clubhead through the ball along the target line on future attempts. If your clubface consistently points right of the target at impact, you will swing the clubhead through the ball from outside to inside the target line (dashed clubhead path), in an instinctive effort to prevent the ball from going to the right. If your clubface consistently points left of target at impact, you will do the opposite — swing through the ball from inside to outside the target line in an instinctive effort to stop the ball from going left (dotted path).

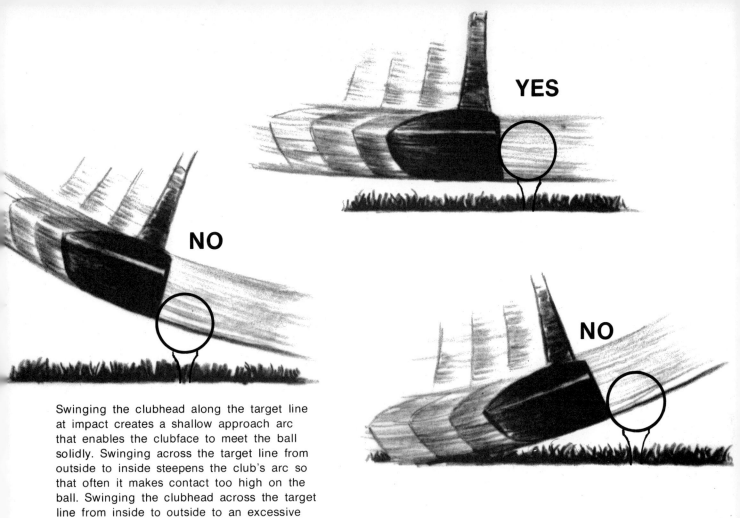

YES

NO

NO

Swinging the clubhead along the target line at impact creates a shallow approach arc that enables the clubface to meet the ball solidly. Swinging across the target line from outside to inside steepens the club's arc so that often it makes contact too high on the ball. Swinging the clubhead across the target line from inside to outside to an excessive degree often causes it to contact the ground before it meets the ball.

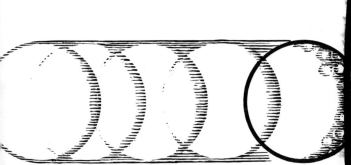

The distance your ball flies is governed not — as so many golfers think — by your clubhead speed alone, but by clubhead speed *squarely applied*. Thus long-hitting is as much a matter of achieving the correct "impact geometry" as using your muscles in a particular way.

why the world is full of golfers who say "I know what to do but I can't do it." They can't do it because, whatever their conscious desires, their actual swing actions are *reactions* to basic major faults.

The thing we all react to most is the face of the club. You must realize — and never forget— that incorrect alignment of the clubface at impact on one shot affects the entire golf swing on the next. Any cure is not to be found in swing "positions." It lies in developing a grip and swing that brings the clubface square to your swing line at impact. Do this and all your reactions will be correct ones. Everything suddenly — and miraculously — falls into place. Now, if you swing from out-to-in, the ball will go to the left. You will immediately, *subconsciously,* make an effort to hit more from inside the target line. Your *natural* adjustment to help you do that will be to pull your body around so that you can swing that way. And — bingo! — suddenly you are set up square instead of open. Now you can swing the club so that it can approach the ball at the right level to hit it solidly in the back. Your shots start straight and fly straight. You've got the "secret"! Fantastic! And not one word about "hit late," "slide your hips," "keep your head down"!

Technically, golf is a much simpler game than most people realize. Here's another way to look at it simply. If you are consistently mishitting and misdirecting the ball, it should cheer you to know that there are only two basic causes. Either:

1. *You have an open clubface at impact,* which makes you swing across the target line from outside to inside, which in turn makes the club descend too steeply into the ball and thus not meet it solidly — or

2. *You have a closed clubface at impact,* which makes you swing across the target line from inside to outside, which makes the clubhead descend too shallowly into the ball, thus either catching the ground behind it or hitting the ball "thin" at the start of the upswing.

The perfect impact occurs only when the clubhead at impact travels exactly along the target line and exactly faces the target. This is "square" — the only "square" in golf. This is your aim — the total objective of all you do with a golf club. What this book is all about.

There's just one more point I must make before we launch off into what I hope you will find an instructive and entertaining book. It is my number two credo as a teacher of golf. It is this: "The art of competing is to know your limitations and to try on every shot."

What this really means is that

the technique of striking the ball — the thing I personally deal in most of the time — is no more than 50 per cent of the game. Temperament, intelligence, nerve, desire and many other mental qualities make up the other 50 per cent. So, when we are talking technique, as we are in the first part of this book, you might like to keep in mind that we are not dealing with the whole game. Unfortunately, even if you can learn to hit it like Jack Nicklaus, you still have to learn to play like him.

Learn–and never forget–golf's basic 'geometry'

If what I said a moment ago makes sense, being able, *yourself,* to analyze errors in your clubface alignment and swing direction from the way your shots behave is obviously an absolute prerequisite to playing better golf.

Learning what I call the "geometry" of the game is a mental, not a practice-ground, process. It isn't difficult, but it involves sitting down and thinking for a few moments.

The behavior of every shot you hit is caused by a specific inter-relationship of the clubface angle and the swing direction at impact. Here is how:

PULL — ball flies on a straight line but to the left of your target
The club's head is traveling across your intended target line from outside to inside that line at impact. The clubface is square to the *line of your swing,* but not to your *target line.* These shots often feel solid even though they fly in the wrong direction. The direction the clubface was looking and clubhead was moving "matched," thus obviating a glancing blow.

SLICE — ball starts left of your target then bends to the right
The club is again traveling across the intended target line from out to in during impact, but this time the face is *open*—facing right — of your swing line. This creates a clockwise sidespin that bends the ball to the right as its forward impetus decreases. The more the clubface and swing path are in opposition, the more oblique the blow, the greater the sidespin and the bigger the slice. Also, the more your swing line is from outside your target line, the steeper will be the club's approach to the ball and the higher up — and thus more glancing — its contact on the ball.

PULLED HOOK — ball starts left of your target, then bends farther to the left
Again, the club is traveling across your intended target line from out to in, but this time the face is *closed* to the line of

19

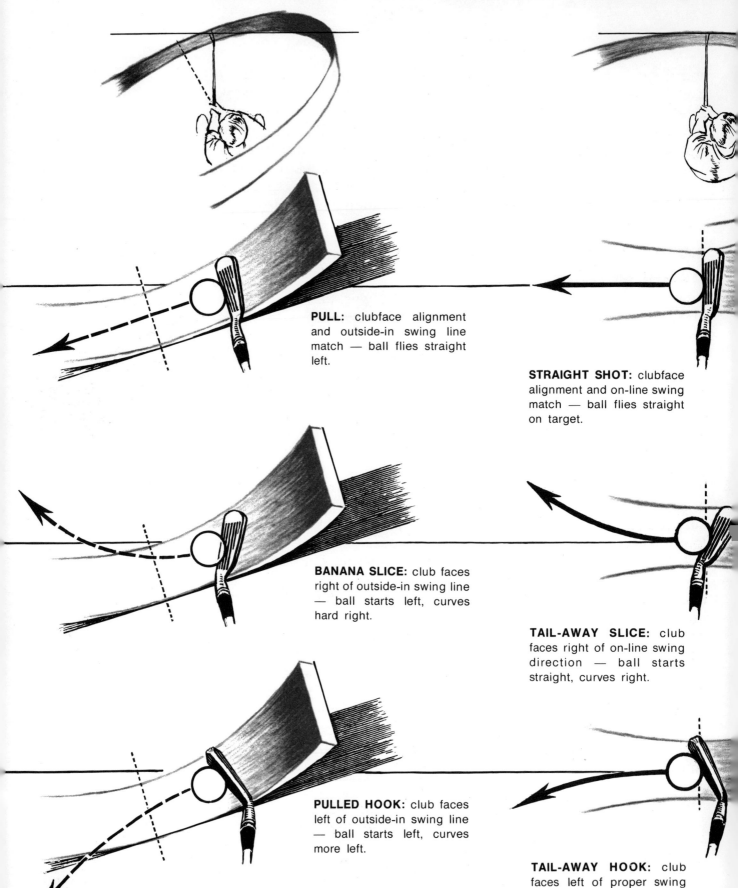

PULL: clubface alignment and outside-in swing line match — ball flies straight left.

STRAIGHT SHOT: clubface alignment and on-line swing match — ball flies straight on target.

BANANA SLICE: club faces right of outside-in swing line — ball starts left, curves hard right.

TAIL-AWAY SLICE: club faces right of on-line swing direction — ball starts straight, curves right.

PULLED HOOK: club faces left of outside-in swing line — ball starts left, curves more left.

TAIL-AWAY HOOK: club faces left of proper swing line — ball starts straight, curves left.

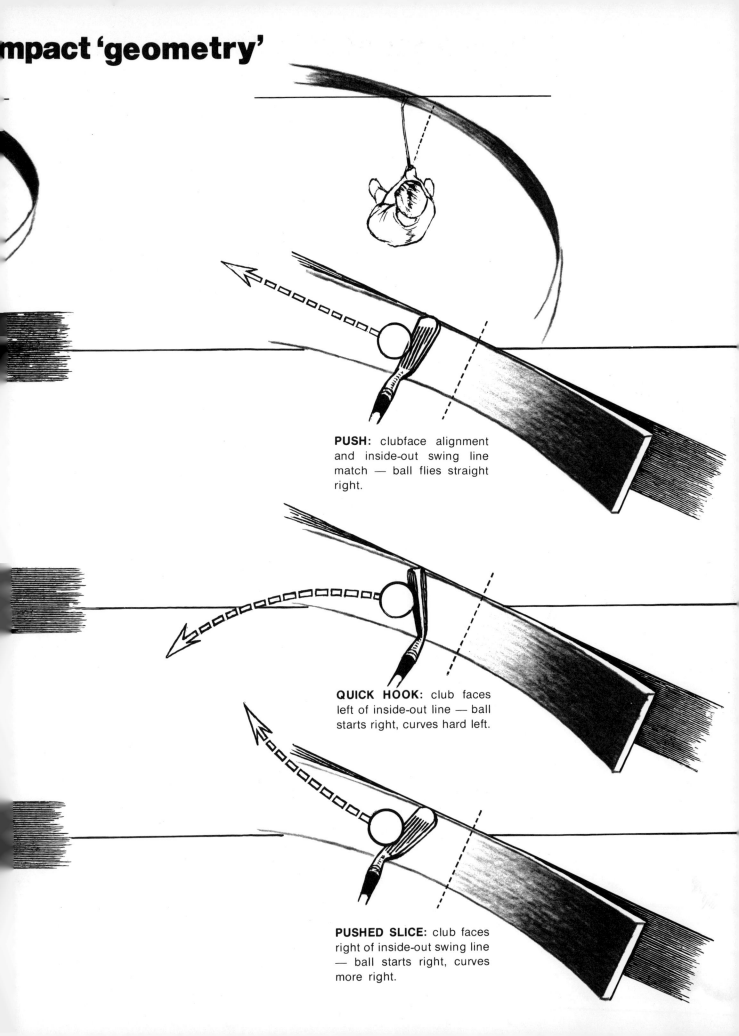

PUSH: clubface alignment and inside-out swing line match — ball flies straight right.

QUICK HOOK: club faces left of inside-out line — ball starts right, curves hard left.

PUSHED SLICE: club faces right of inside-out swing line — ball starts right, curves more right.

swing. This combination of two faults in the same direction sends the ball disastrously to the left — the infamous "smothered hook."

PUSH — ball flies straight but to the right of your target

Again, the clubhead is traveling across your intended target line at impact, but this time from in to out. Your clubface is square to your line of swing, but *not* to your target line. Obviously the ball flies where both the clubface and swing path direct it — to the right. As with the pull, this shot often feels solid, because the blow is not of the glancing variety.

HOOK — ball starts right of your target, then bends to the left

The club is again traveling across your intended line from in to out, but this time the face is *closed*, facing left of the line of your swing. This creates counter-clockwise sidespin that bends the ball left once its forward impetus decreases. Unless the clubhead's angle of approach is so low that it hits the ground before it gets to the ball, a hooked shot feels much more solidly struck than a slice. This is because the clubface, by moving parallel to the ground instead of sharply downward, contacts the back-center of the ball, not its top as in a slice.

PUSHED SLICE — ball starts right of your target then bends more to the right

Again, the club is traveling across your intended target line from in to out at impact, but this time the face is *open* to the line of your swing. These two faults combining in the same direction send the ball devastatingly far right.

STRAIGHT SHOT — Ball starts straight and flies straight along your target line

The clubface looks at the target and your swing line coincides with the target line at impact.

You are now able to analyze your own swing, and I hope you will at last appreciate what "analyze" really means in golfing terms. It doesn't mean standing in front of a mirror and trying to spot whether your left knee bends inwards or forwards, whether your left arm is straight or bent at the top, etc., etc. You can make a complete analysis of your swing while you shave, sit in a train, ride to the office, or lie in bed. *All you have to do is think about the way your golf ball reacts when you hit it.*

It is obvious that, if you hook a lot, you'll probably also push the ball because these two shapes are a *swing-path pair*. Both require a swing-path that is in-to-out during impact. Conversely, if you slice you will also pull, because these two shapes are the other *swing-path pair* (out-to-in).

Every golfer belongs to one of these categories. His offline shots will *start out* consistently left or right of the target line. A big bending of the shot, left or right, is dependent on the direction his clubface was looking, relative to his swing line during impact. A closed-clubface golfer will be a hooker who pushes the ball when he happens to return the clubface in the same direction he's swinging. An open-clubface golfer will be a slicer who pulls when he happens to return the clubface in the same direction *he* is swinging.

Want to be sure of your category? Here's how to find out.

First, take a driver to the practice ground and hit half a dozen shots. If they bend from left to right in the air, the clubface is open to your swing line at impact. If they curve the other way the clubface is closed. By using a club with very little loft, you will always get an honest picture of your clubface alignment at impact. Why? Because, since the club's loft is minimal, little backspin is created by a back-of-the-ball blow — too little, in fact, to override the sidespin imparted by the oblique contact of an open or shut clubface.

Next, take a nine-iron and hit a few more shots. Because of its greater loft, this club contacts the *bottom* back of the ball, imparting heavy backspin. Consequently, the influence of sidespin is reduced to the point where the direction in which the ball flies accurately reflects the path of your swing. For example, you will almost certainly hit the highly-lofted clubs straight, but left, if you are a slicer with the driver.

Before we leave golf's "geometry" — although it will be constantly referred to in this book — there are a couple more factors I'd like you to understand.

The first is that your club needs to swing *along* the target line only just before, during and just after impact — a *matter of a few inches.* You *do not,* as some books suggest, have to swing it along the target line a number of feet in order to hit the ball straight. This leads directly to another point I'd like to clarify. You stand *inside* the arc you make with the club. The only way, therefore, that you can swing the club straight along the target line is to have it coming into the ball from *inside* the target line. Once the clubhead passes outside the target line in the downswing, it cannot swing along this line during impact, *but only back across it.*

By the same token, if your club is to follow a true arc, it will quickly move *inside* the target line again after you have struck the ball. Thus the clubhead path of a golf swing that hits the ball straight is not, as many people seem to believe, inside to out. *It is in-*

side, to straight-through, to inside again. We will go further into this much-misunderstood piece of "geometry" in discussing the mechanics of the actual swing.

Should you SWING, or move from position to position?

Should you really *swing* the club? Or should you merely move through a series of contrived postures, a pattern of carefully thought-out conscious movements, a set of deliberate muscle contortions? The question may seem silly but it is of prime importance, especially if you are new to the game or have never achieved the golfing prowess of which you feel yourself potentially capable.

A Rolls Royce without an engine might look impressive, but it's never going to get out of the garage. In exactly the same way, a golf swing without an engine, however beautifully contoured each part might be, is never going to move the ball very far out of your shadow. To do that your swing, whatever else it lacks, must have power, motivation. **It must be a swing.** In the simplest of golfing terms, you must "hit the ball."

Am I stating the obvious? I think not. Using "swing" in its literal sense, I believe golfers today don't *swing* as well as they did 30 years ago. They might score as well, or better, but this is not necessarily due to playing technique. Course conditions and golf equipment, plus the mental attitudes prevalent in sport today, have had big effects on the game.

If it is true that we don't *swing* as well as our fathers did, the main reason seems to me to be our growing predilection with what I call "static golf."

Most of the great golfers up to a decade or two ago learned the game as caddies. They watched the people they carried for and tried to copy those who played well. They were copying an action, a fluid movement, as was the pupil of the old-time professional, whose lesson consisted chiefly of demonstration. It would never have occurred to most old pros, even if they had known how, to break the swing down into parts and study it segment by segment in static form. Golf was **action**, and was learned as such.

The development of the camera and high-speed film, plus man's uncontrollable urge for self-analysis, changed all this. It was thought that if the golf swing could be "stopped" inch by inch and studied, we could learn all about it. But, even in the earliest days of golf photography, this proved less practicable than it seemed theoretically. Camera analysis soon proved that even star performers were, in fact, not doing what they thought they were doing; or doing what they thought they were not doing. (I seem to remember this being especially true of Harry Vardon, upon whom once all the world modelled its golf. Photography proved that some of the things he believed he did in striking a golf ball so perfectly did not, in fact, take place. Throwing the club from the top — as if casting a fishing rod — was one of them.)

Nevertheless, the camera played an increasingly large part in the exploration of golf technique, with the result that today a great many people tend to learn golf as a "static" game rather than as a game of movement. Instead of watching good players in the flesh, and trying to emulate the *action* of a good golf swing, they study static pictures and try to copy the positions in which the camera has frozen the player.

Before the age of stop-action photography, most good players learned the game by copying a *swing.* They were not concerned generally with the positions which enabled them to apply the clubhead to the ball, but with the *action* by which they did so. The positional stuff — the controlling of the swing — came much later.

It seems to me that the mod-ern golfer trying to learn golf from static pictures — especially if he has no other form of instruction — is doing the job backwards. He is learning positions which, in themselves, without the essential motivating force of swinging, are almost useless.

This does not mean to say that the very excellent "action" photographs published in golf magazines and books are of no value in learning the game. Golf involves two static positions at the outset — the grip and the set-up — and pictures are of great benefit in teaching these. They can also be valuable in helping people to better control and direct the swing — *once they have a swing to control.* It is when the swing has never been installed, or has run down or is misfiring, that "positional" golf, book-lore, is of limited value.

Undoubtedly, the biggest danger in "static" golf, in learning from still pictures, is that body action becomes overemphasized. Photographs cannot show "motion," but they show very well how the body changes position during the golf swing. It is these positional impressions that the beginner and the poor golfer is apt to copy and frequently to overdo.

Some years ago, when I first went to Rome to teach Italian assistants how to teach golf, I found that all of them were teaching body action. Most were ex-caddies who had played from an early age and hit the ball quite well naturally. In other words, all of them had developed *swings* without ever thinking about it. When they did come to study the golf swing cerebrally, it was body movement that seemed of prime importance, so they taught that, never realizing that their pupils were people who had not developed the motivating forces that become automatic for anyone who plays the game from early youth.

I pointed out to them — as I do to pupils daily — that to *swing* is the first priority, the absolute pre-requisite of good golf. Indeed, a swing of the arms alone will produce great golf, even with the most unorthodox body action or positioning. Just think of all the great players there have been over the years with unorthodox movements.

Obviously, then, if your golf is not all you'd like it to be, and especially if you are an eager theoretician, it might be worth overhauling the basic motivating force, the "engine" of your swing. More often than not you'll be surprised at the improvement that results from getting back to the basic precept of golf — using the arms, wrists and hands to propel the clubhead through the ball *fast*.

In doing this with a pupil, or

in teaching a beginner, I have an order of procedure that you also might like to follow.

First of all, I explain and make sure that the player understands the true function of the grip. Once this has sunk home, we have generally gone a long way towards making or improving a golfer. I then pass on to the set-up, and again try to make clear the purpose of standing in a certain way before actually getting a pupil to do so.

Once he comprehends the true purposes (and has to some degree mastered the mechanics) of grip and stance, any person will play reasonable golf who understands and "feels," at the outset, that the club must be *swung* up and then down *through* the ball. One of my most frequent teaching phrases comes to mind: "Set it up and set it off, and the club will largely do it for you."

The golf *swing* is largely a *natural* action. Yet all over the world golf courses are full of people trying to play the game who have never learned this basic fact, or whose preoccupation with the more abstruse mechanics of the game has made them lose sight of the importance of simply *swinging*.

The great challenge for many teachers today — due, I am sure, to our preoccupation with "static" golf — is to get these golfers to simply propel the ball with the clubhead, and to stop them trying to hit it with their bodies. Body action is important in golf, but is *complementary* to the swinging of the clubhead, not the dominating factor of the swing. The body movement must be in sympathy with the clubhead as controlled by the hands, not try to take over from the clubhead the function of striking the ball.

The easiest way to learn golf is by instinct and by copying. When I teach groups of young children for the Golf Foundation, I do very little talking, but I never stop swinging. And they learn — how quickly they learn! Unfortunately, we lose this imitative ability as we grow older, and it becomes necessary to learn golf more by reason — to master the game cerebrally.

This can be done, but how well depends entirely on the instinct to *swing*— rather than maneuver — the club that is already in operation, or can be built up to motivate our mentally-inspired mechanical efforts.

I think I could put the point in a nut-shell by saying that body action can never be a substitute for arm and hand action, but that, once a free swing is developed, good body action is essential to groove and control it — to keep the swing on track. Body action — control — possibly can be learned from static pictures. But for the club to swing down and forward at over 100 m.p.h., the arms must *swing*. Arm and hand action also promote "feel," and this too can only be learned by *swinging*.

THE SWING

Your grip determines how you play

If clubface alignment at impact is golf's critical "geometrical" factor, then how the golfer holds his club — and thus controls this alignment — is the supreme factor determining the success or failure of his shots.

Much as many golfers would like to be able to ignore this fact, it is inescapable. The old saw, that you never see a good golfer with a bad grip or a bad golfer with a good grip, is pretty true. Whether you are a beginner or a seasoned player seeking improvement, finding a grip *that naturally returns the club-face square to your swing line* is your absolute first priority; your inescapable starting point. If you are an established golfer, but feel you have never reached your full potential at the game, it is a 5-to-1 chance that your grip is at the root of your problems.

The majority of golfers *never* develop a proper grip. Quite naturally, they want to get on with hitting the ball. They regard the way they hold the club as a minor and relatively boring aspect of the game, compared to the fascinating technical intricasies of the swing itself. Even if they do make an effort to develop a correct grip, few persevere because any change feels so uncomfortable at first. I hate to preach, but this is a cart-before-horse approach that will *always* limit you as a golfer. If you want to play to the maximum of your potential, you *must* develop a correct grip.

What is a correct grip?

First, I want you to forget anything you have read or heard that suggests that there is one, and only one, way to hold a golf club. Everybody has a correct grip, but finding it is not a matter of arranging the hands on the club in a standard position, as so many books and teachers suggest. It is a matter of finding the grip that enables *you* (not Arnold Palmer nor Jack Nicklaus nor Tony Jacklin) *to face your club in the direction you are swinging it at impact, while swinging at speed.*

At the risk of laboring the point, I repeat: it is to make this possible — and only this — that the golf club is held in a particular way.

Down the long history of golf, a certain pattern of placing the hands and fingers on the club has been found to make returning the clubhead square to the swing line at speed easiest for the greatest number of people. Let's look at this basic system first, then at the variations you may need to adopt to suit your own physical make-up.

To start with, you place the club diagonally in your open left hand, so that it lies in the crook of the first finger and across the

Pattern your grip thus.....

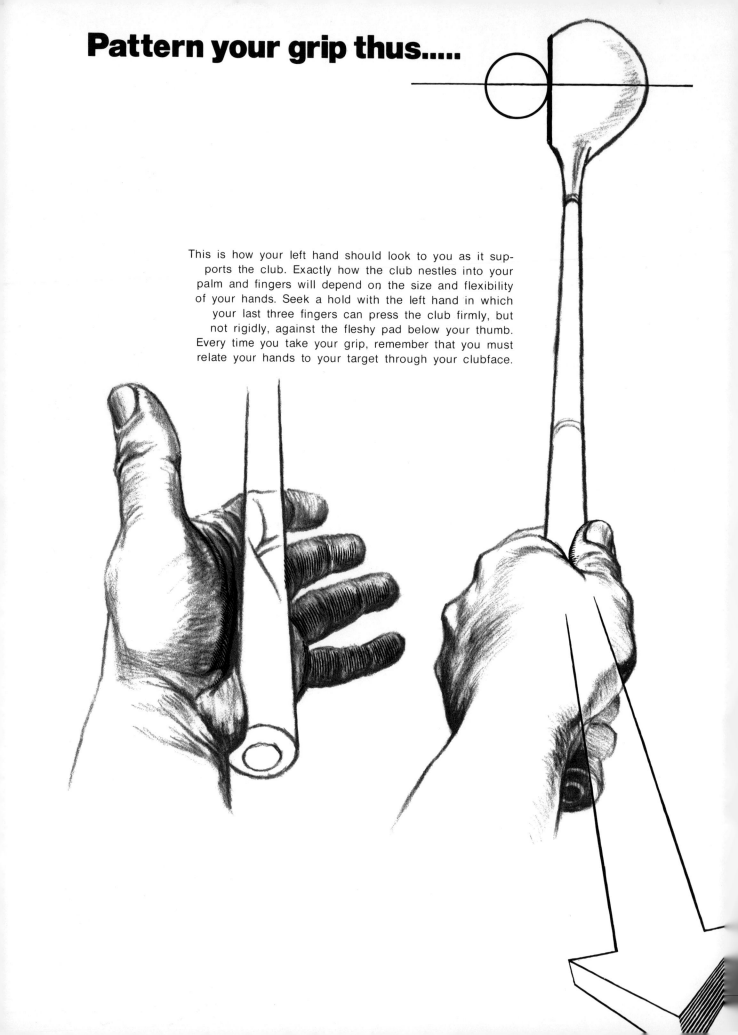

This is how your left hand should look to you as it supports the club. Exactly how the club nestles into your palm and fingers will depend on the size and flexibility of your hands. Seek a hold with the left hand in which your last three fingers can press the club firmly, but not rigidly, against the fleshy pad below your thumb. Every time you take your grip, remember that you must relate your hands to your target through your clubface.

The club will naturally sit a little more in the fingers of your right hand than it does in your left, and you will probably secure the club most comfortably by holding it firmly, but not tightly, with your two middle fingers. "Wrap" your right hand snugly against your left, so that the pad below your right thumb caresses the top of your left thumb. By more-or-less matching the direction of the "Vs" formed by your thumbs and forefingers, you set your hands parallel to each other, which encourages them to work as a unit during the swing.

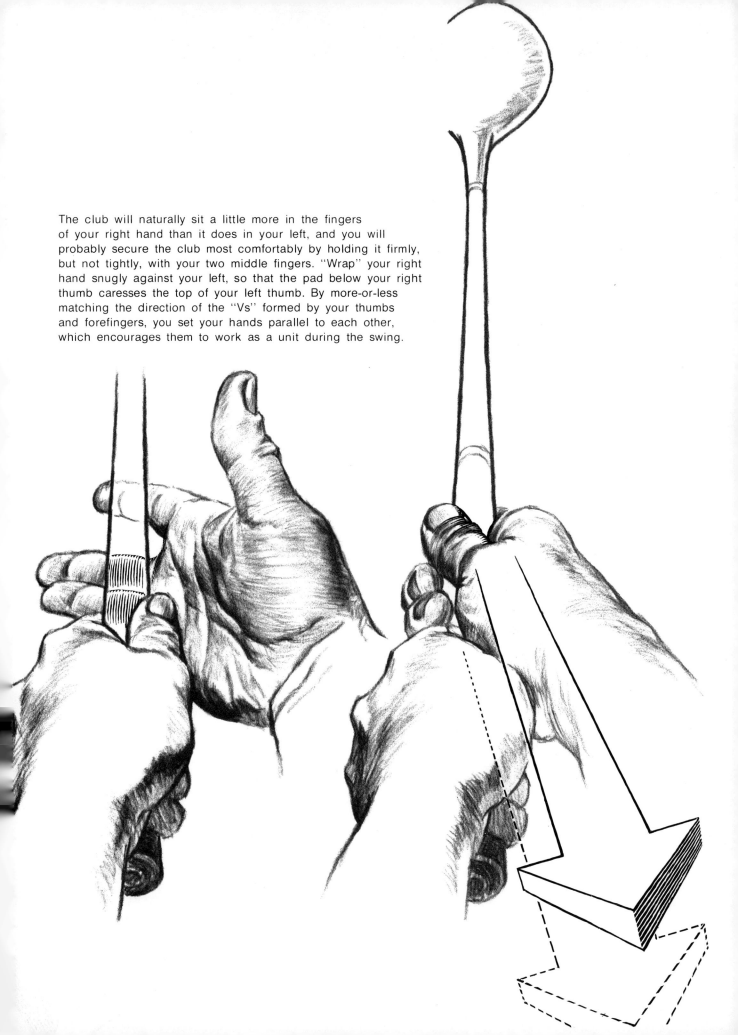

NORMAL

WEAK

STRONG

...but experiment between these extremes to discover what works for you.

The correct grip for you is the one that delivers your clubface square to your direction of swing during impact. The grip pattern that does that for Jack Nicklaus or Lee Trevino may not do it for you, so face up to the need for some experiment. This will probably be uncomfortable at first, but if you skip it you can forget ever becoming a good golfer, because your repeated misalignment of the clubface at impact will *consistently* create faults in your set-up and swing. Start with your "Vs" pointing to "Normal" — midway between your nose and your right shoulder. If the flight of your shots tells you that you are delivering the clubface to the ball looking to the right of your swing line, move both your hands gradually towards the "Strong" position. If your shots tell you that the clubface is arriving at the ball looking left of your swing path, move both "Vs" gradually towards the "Weak" position. Your grip is right for *you* when your shots fly straight, even though you may be pulling the ball right or pushing it left of target. No curve on your shots shows that your clubface alignment and swing direction are matched.

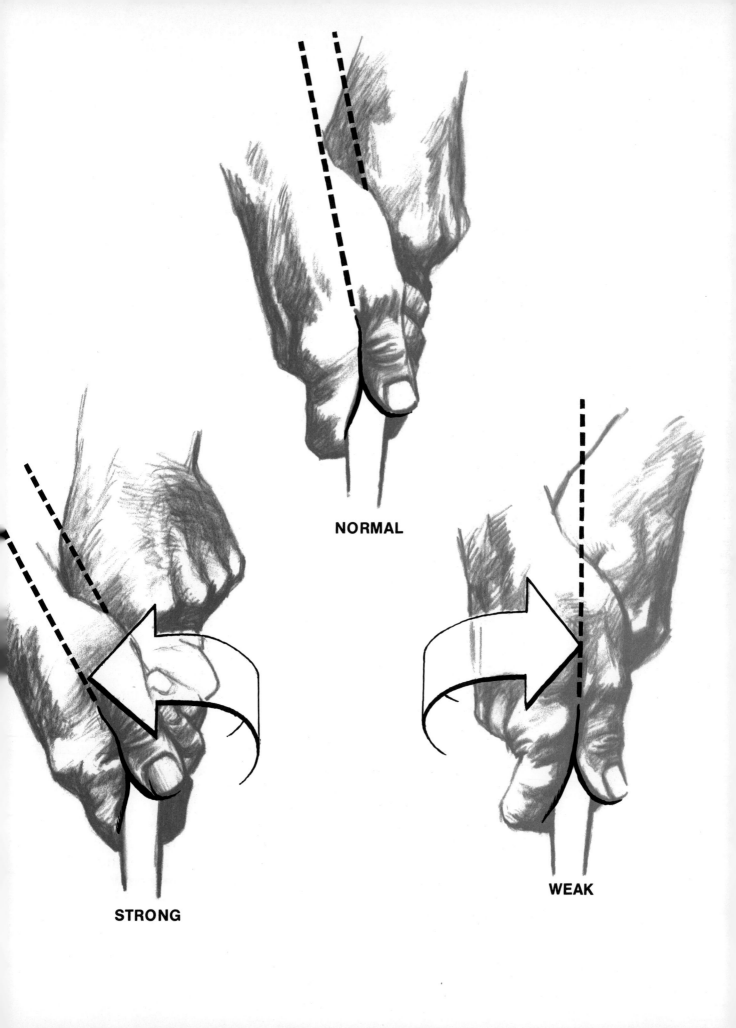

NORMAL

STRONG

WEAK

palm under the butt of your thumb. Next, you close this hand over the shaft, with the left thumb riding just to the right side of the shaft. If you do this properly, you will find that you are holding the club with your last three fingers pushing it firmly against your palm; and that the "V" formed by the thumb and forefinger is pointing more or less at your right shoulder when you ground the club with its face square to your target. You will also probably find, looking down, that you can see between two and three knuckles of your left hand.

Next you add your right hand to your grip, by bringing it onto the shaft as close as is comfortably possible to your left hand, in such a way that the palm is pretty much parallel to the palm of your left hand. You should find that the shaft nestles down snugly into the roots of the fingers of your right hand, and that your are gripping the club predominantly with the second and third fingers of this hand. Next, check that your right thumb is slightly on the left side of the shaft; that your left thumb snuggles cosily against the palm of your right hand; and that your right forefinger is "triggered" easily around the shaft.

If it helps to make your hands more of a single unit, wrap the little finger of your right hand around the forefinger of your left (called the overlapping grip); or slip it between the forefinger and second finger of your left hand (called the interlocking grip). Finally, check that the "V" formed by the thumb and forefinger of your right hand points roughly to the same spot as the left hand "V". This will ensure that your palms are pretty well parallel, which will greatly facilitate your hands working smoothly together as a single unit.

That, then, is the *basic* grip. For the majority of golfers it is, with minor modifications, the way of holding the club that will most effectively allow them to return the clubface square to the ball at speed.

But there are those for whom such a grip pattern will *not* work. Because of age, unusual muscular strength or weakness, flexibility or playing frequency, this "orthodox" grip will not *automatically* swing the clubface through the ball looking in the same direction as the club is moving. It will either be open or closed to the swing line, causing sliced or hooked shots. Whenever this happens, the golfer must experiment intelligently within the above framework, to find the modification *he personally needs* to square his clubface to his swing line.

If he is a chronic slicer, almost certainly he will need to reposition his grip, little by little, until he is at least sure that, whatever other faults he possesses, the clubface is not open to the swing line when it meets the ball. This involves positioning both hands, *as a unit,* more to the right — so that the "Vs" point to the outside of the right shoulder at address, with maybe three knuckles of the left hand showing.

If he is a hooker — the strong golfer's fault — he will most probably need to adopt more the type of hold on the club used by the majority of top professionals, who spend their lives controlling a tendency to hook shots. This involves the exact opposite of the slicer's modification, i.e., gradually positioning both hands more to the left, so that the "Vs" point, say, to the right eye, and only one or maybe one-and-a-half knuckles are visible.

That's really all there is to be said about the grip. It isn't complicated — it's just *vital* that you go out and work and think and experiment to find *your* correct grip within the framework I've explained to achieve the objective I've stated. When you have done that, you have mastered 50 per cent of striking the ball well. And if you can add a good set-up to an effective grip, you'll have mastered 90 per cent.

Set up so you can swing the club on target

Let's assume that you're now holding the club in such a way that at impact it faces more often than not in the same direction it is traveling. The ball now flies fairly straight, but its straight-line flight is still to the left of your target.

What are you going to do to get the ball to finish on target? Well, what's the *instinctive* thing to do? Yes, that's right — you've got it! You are going to shift yourself around more to the right at address, because *instinctively* you know this will help you to swing the club along the target line at impact.

That, in one sentence, is set-up. Your grip determines where your clubface looks at impact. Where you aim yourself at address largely determines in which direction you'll swing the club through the ball. Just simple common sense, isn't it? And yet, not five golfers in a hundred approach the job this way. The reason, I believe, is that setting-up correctly, like gripping correctly, is a "static" procedure, and as such bores most golfers. Everybody wants to rush into action, preferably with a driver. Yet, even Ben Hogan's superb swing would not have got him round the course inside 80 if he hadn't aimed his shots correctly before he moved the club. How in the name of heaven do *you*

35

Set up to set off the correct chain reaction

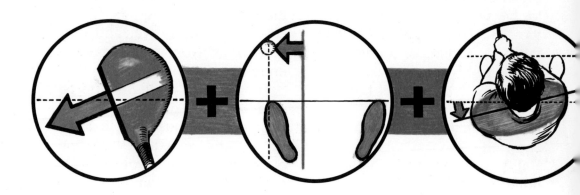

Here's the chain reaction of set-up errors that continues to frustrate a golfer who repeatedly strikes shots with a closed clubface. Instinctively he aims the clubface right of target at address, to stop the ball finishing left. This causes him to position the ball too far back in his stance. Addressing the ball so far back pulls the golfer's shoulders into a closed position — aimed right of his target (even though, again, his feet may be positioned square to the target line). The closed alignment of his shoulders establishes a "strong" grip relative to the target line — his hands are turned too far to his right.

The cumulative effect of these faults — again born of instinct — is to perpetuate the hooking tendency. The golfer's strong grip delivers the clubface closed to his clubhead path. His closed shoulders and rearward ball positioning force him to swing the clubhead acutely from in to out across the target line. The ball starts right but spins strongly to the left. When the golfer does square the clubface to his in-to-out swing path, the ball flies straight but right of his target (push.)

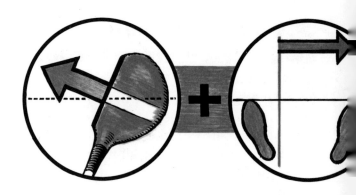

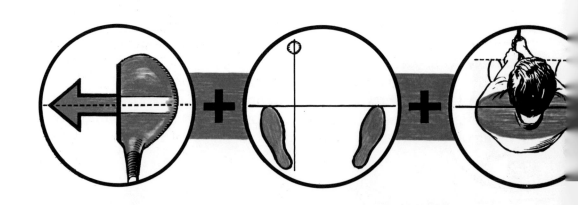

By reacting instinctively rather than analytically to the flight of their shots, golfers set off chain-reactions of errors. Here is the chain-reaction of frustrating set-up faults that develops from repeatedly contacting the ball with the clubface open (facing right of the path on which it is moving.) In an instinctive effort to prevent the ball slicing to the right of his target, the golfer aims his clubface left of target at address. This encourages positioning the ball too far forward in his stance. Addressing the ball so far forward pulls the shoulders open — aligning them left of the target (even though the golfer's feet may be square to his target line). The open-shoulder alignment encourages the golfer to place his hands too much on top of the club, setting them in a "slicer's" grip relative to his target line. The cumulative effect of these faults — bred, remember, by an *instinctive* attempt to stop the ball curving right — is to further encourage slicing. The golfer's weak grip returns his clubface open to his swing-path. His open shoulders and forward ball positioning force him to deliver the clubhead to the ball while it is traveling across his target line, from out-to-in. Struck with a cutting blow, the ball starts left and spins weakly to the right. If the golfer squares his clubface to his out-to-in swing path, the ball will fly straight left of his target (pull).

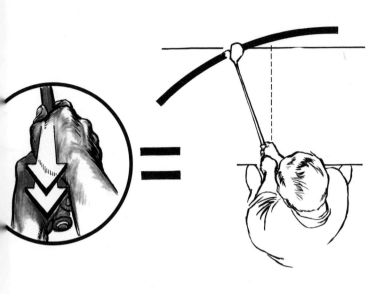

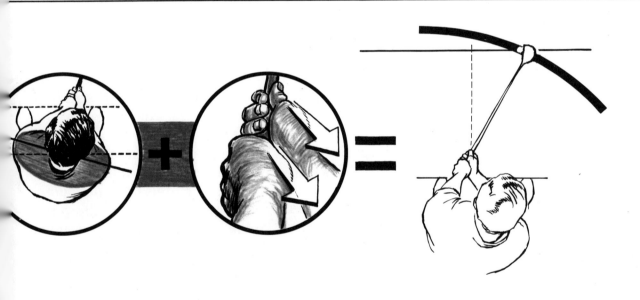

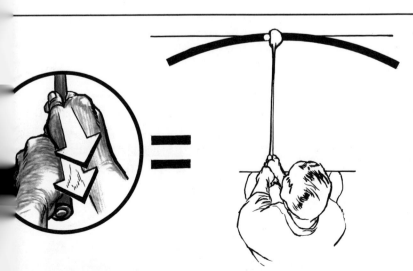

Here's the correct set-up chain-reaction. The golfer aims the clubface squarely at his target. With the clubhead facing correctly and lying flat on the ground, the correct ball position relative to the feet is established by the angle of the club's shaft when the golfer squares his shoulders to his target line. Square shoulder alignment enables the golfer to correctly "match" his grip to both his clubface and his target line. Thus he becomes ideally set-up to swing the clubhead through the ball along — rather than across — the target line, with the face looking in the same direction the clubhead is traveling.

expect to?

"Set-up" is a phrase for aim and posture (or stance, if you prefer it). Its purpose is to establish the best possible chance of swinging the club along the target line at impact. Actually, getting set-up correctly involves an exact and almost ritualized procedure. (Watch the top pros at any big tournament if you don't believe me). That procedure is as follows:

1. You grip the club correctly for *you,* as we have already spelled out.

2. Maintaining that correct grip, you aim the club correctly by placing it behind the ball *so that its bottom edge is exactly at right angles to your target.*

3. Having gripped and aimed the club correctly, you arrange your body and limbs in the position that most easily and naturally allows you to **swing along the line established by the aim of the clubface.** This means simply that you stand with your shoulders, chest, hips, knees and feet at right angles — or "square" — to the clubface; or, to put it another way, parallel to your target line. You stand parallel to the line you want your club to be swinging along in the vital impact area.

Every time I stand by a first tee I get a tremendous urge to implant this simple idea of set-up in the people driving off, just to see the expression on their faces at the 50 per cent im-

provement that would immediately occur in their shot-making. I know that if I could find a foolproof way of getting them to do it right every time, I'd be a millionaire in a month!

It's because set-up is so vital that I prefer to teach people in pairs or small groups. They may not believe what they are doing, or what I tell them they are doing, but when they actually see a friend doing it too, they are usually convinced. Aim and stance control the direction of the swing, and it is always easier to put over such principles of "cause and effect" with a group of pupils, simply because each person involuntarily proves the point to the others. For this reason it is worthwhile, if you have a friend of about the same ability, to take lessons together and play and practice together. Professionals do this all the time, because, when the really good golfer is out of form, it is most often because he has slipped out of his correct starting position, which rapidly leads him into all kinds of swing compensations. The bad golfer never gets into a good starting position, except perhaps by accident, which explains his infrequent good shots.

It's this simple: a good set-up makes a good golf swing and thus a good shot very probable; a bad set-up makes either highly improbable.

Getting back to specifics, it is vital, **for each and every shot**, to set the clubhead behind the ball with its face precisely at right angles to your desired line of flight. Most people start out wrongly here. Looking along the line of the shot, they stick their feet in what they believe to be the right position, and **then** they dump the clubhead down behind the ball. It could be pointing anywhere, and generally is.

It is essential to get the clubhead down behind the ball **first**, not only so you can aim yourself relative to it, but to ensure that the ball is in the correct position relative to your feet.

Positioning the feet first causes bad ball positioning as well as incorrect aim, because the club, when finally grounded, can be either too far to your left (forward) or too far to your right (rearward). If the ball is too far forward in your stance, your shoulders are dragged round to aim left of target, causing that old out-to-in clubhead path through impact. If the ball (and thus the club) are too far right, the shoulders tend to align to the right of target, promoting an exaggerated in-to-out swing.

It's worth also noting here that hand-action, the key to powerful shot-making, tends to break down any time the set-up is poor. If you are swinging out-to-in (the ball starts to the left) your hand-action will be blocked by the action of your shoulders twisting. If you are the other way (too far right and thus in-to-out), your hand-action will become a wrist-roll in the hitting area. Remember that the hands nearly always do the *instinctive* thing; if you swing out-to-in they will restrain the clubhead, leave its face open, and thus slice the ball; if you swing in-to-out they will roll the clubface closed and produce a hook.

Many golfers have genuine difficulty in aligning themselves parallel to their target line. I find they need some kind of gimmick, a checking device, and here's one of the best. Imagine that your target is down the far rail of a straight piece of railway track. If you now stand on the near rail, with the ball more or less equi-distant between your feet, and lean forward so that you can place the clubhead behind the ball, with its face pointing exactly down the rail, you will be set-up perfectly "square." In other words, your body will be parallel to the rails, and at right angles to your clubface.

Another way to constantly check your set-up is to remember that the first part of the flight of the ball — its trajectory before side-spin affects its flight — indicates the direction in which you were swinging the club at impact. For instance, if

Aim before you fire

Most golfers are so eager to pull the trigger they forget to aim the gun. Even a perfect swing won't send the ball to its target if your clubhead alignment and clubhead path are out of whack. Addressing the ball is a ritualized procedure with all good golfers, because they know that nine-tenths of accurate shot-making rests with the proper grip and set-up. Step 1 in the set-up procedure is to grip the club correctly, as you start to move yourself into position. Step 2 is to place the clubhead behind the ball so that its face looks directly at your target. Step 3 is to move yourself into position so that your body (especially your shoulders) align squarely to your clubface and thus parallel to your target line. Proper aiming is easy because you are still "static." But if you can't be bothered with such preliminaries, don't expect to fire in the desired direction too often.

Posture is important

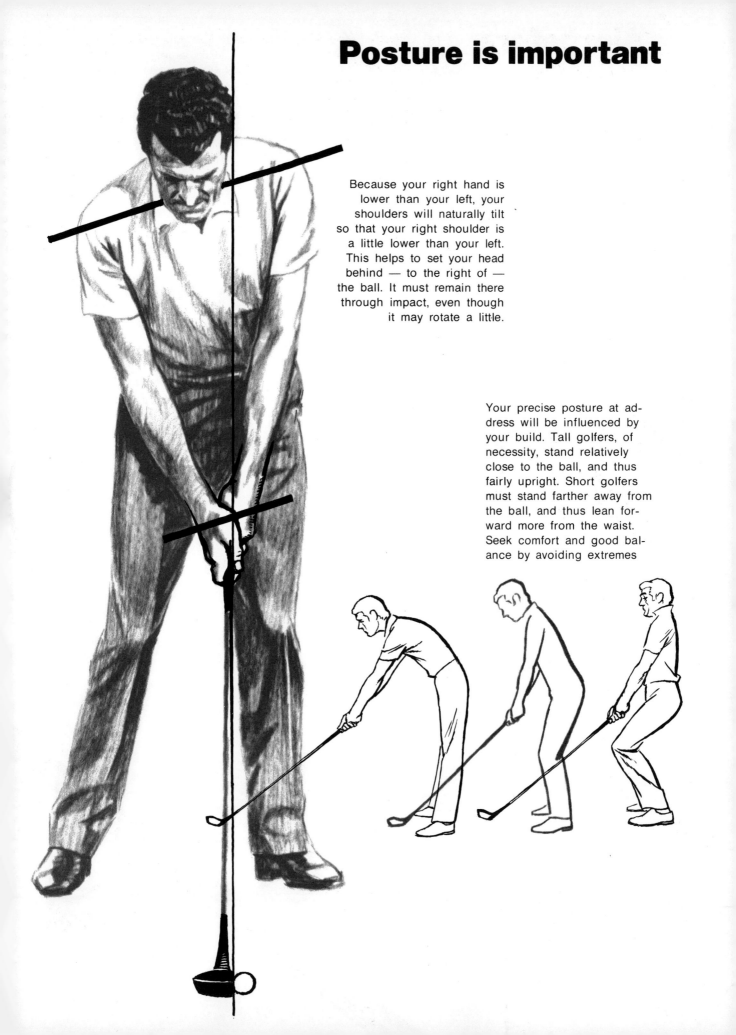

Because your right hand is lower than your left, your shoulders will naturally tilt so that your right shoulder is a little lower than your left. This helps to set your head behind — to the right of — the ball. It must remain there through impact, even though it may rotate a little.

Your precise posture at address will be influenced by your build. Tall golfers, of necessity, stand relatively close to the ball, and thus fairly upright. Short golfers must stand farther away from the ball, and thus lean forward more from the waist. Seek comfort and good balance by avoiding extremes

Getting it all on track

Picturing a golfer standing on one track of a railroad to hit a ball sitting on the other track is one of the most popular teaching analogies. It is used so often because it so perfectly conveys the ideal of aligning one's body parallel to the target line. Such a set-up encourages swinging the clubhead through the ball along — rather than across — the target line. Also note the posture: the golfer bends from the waist with his back straight. His arms hang free and easy. His knees are slightly flexed. Overall his posture conveys a sense of readiness and resilience.

the ball consistently flies left to start, you are probably aiming too much to the left. If the ball consistently starts right, you are aligned too far right.

The actual posture of the body in setting-up to a full shot is largely controlled by the requirements of aiming properly. The first priority, if you want to hit the ball straight, in the simplest manner, is that your *shoulders* are parallel to the target line when the clubhead is placed squarely behind the ball. Many good golfers play from open or closed positions of the feet, but almost all good players address the ball for normal shots with the shoulders and torso pretty much parallel to the target line.

Because the right hand is lower than the left on the club, the right shoulder should set-up lower than the left. This produces a slight tilt of the upper body to the right, which in turn places your head **behind** the ball. (And here it must **remain** until after impact, even though it may turn on its own axis a little during the swing.) Unless you are so tilted, it will be difficult to swing the club straight through on target. Indeed, setting the right side too high at address is one of the game's commonest faults. It is essential to swing the right shoulder down and under. If it is not set in this position at address, if it is high in relation to the left side, it will

tend instead to swing over and around.

To give your arms room to swing past your body, you must lean forward. This bend should always be from the **waist,** and it should be just enough to allow your arms to hang easily and naturally from your shoulders. Don't reach and don't crouch. Flex your knees into the sort of position you assume as you are just about to sit down, keep your back straight, and incline yourself **comfortably** forward from the waist. Keep your left arm straight, **but not stiff.** Keep your right arm "soft" and let it bend a bit at the elbow, which will point to your right hip.

My final point on the mechanics of set-up is an important one. Most of the power and much of the control in a golf swing depends on coiling the upper body around a resisting base — "winding the spring." Coiling depends upon one end of the spring being anchored. So, as the final check-point before you start to swing the club, make sure that your feet are firmly planted on the ground, that your knees are springily flexed, and that you are in good balance. In short, that your lower half can "resist" the turning of your top half.

Grip and set-up are inseparable and indispensable. As "statics," I know they are boring to most people. But if you won't attend to them, you'll always be a hacker. Get them right and you are 90 per cent of the way to hitting a golf ball to the best of your natural ability.

Know the 'shape' your swing should have—and why

What is the backswing for?

How many golfers, I wonder, have ever asked themselves that question? They know all the things they are supposed to do to make a good backswing — "head still," "shoulders turned 90 degrees, hips turned 45 degrees," "left arm straight," "right elbow tucked in," "transfer the weight," and so on. But have they ever stopped to ask themselves just what it's all *for:* what is the real purpose of the golf backswing?

In case you haven't, I want now to tell you.

The backswing has two purposes. One, the obvious one, is to provide power through the wind-up, or torque-like action, of the body. Its second purpose — perhaps less evident, nearly as important — is a matter of simple geometry, of two vital angles — swing plane and club direction. Assuming you have a grip that returns the face of the club correctly, golf would be a simple game if you could always get these two angles correct.

Theoretically, of course, the ideal swing plane would be vertical — the ultimate in upright swings — because this would eliminate any divergence of the clubhead from the target line. Unfortunately, such a swing is anatomically impossible. Even if it were possible, it would create problems in another dimension — the angle of the clubhead's approach to the ball. Too upright a swing produces too sharp an angle of attack of the club on the ball, creating a weak glancing blow — a "choppy" action.

Thus, since we are endeavoring to propel the ball forward, the ideal plane for the clubhead to travel is a happy medium roughly half-way between vertical (totally upright) and horizontal (totally flat). This is the plane on which most of the world's best golfers swing the club — certainly through impact.

Now, let's look at plane in terms of *your* game.

The plane on which you swing is established chiefly by your address position. As you stand to the ball comfortably and squarely, neither cramped nor reaching, your left arm and club form a more-or-less continuous straight line. The angle of that line relative to the vertical is the "ideal" plane on which to swing the club up and down with your arms.

What you are aiming to do, in golfing terms, is to shift your right side out of the way in the backswing and your left side out of the way on the through-swing, so that at the moment of impact the club is being swung freely by your arms with the clubhead moving straight through the ball, along the target line. To do this a golfer of shortish stature will normally have to stand fairly well away from the ball, and will *naturally* turn his body on a fairly flat plane — at a fairly rotary angle, as do, for example, Ben Hogan and Lee Trevino. A tall golfer, on the other hand, usually needs to stand nearer to the ball, and will *naturally* tilt his body on a more upright plane — less "round himself" and more "underneath himself" like Jack Nicklaus and George Archer.

The shoulders, of course, must also turn on some kind of plane. Should the shoulder-turn plane match the arm-swing plane? Despite what you may have heard or read, or thought to have seen in good golfers, the answer is no. The shoulders should *always* turn on a more horizontal—flatter—plane than the plane of the arm-club swing: (a) to allow the club to reach a top-of-the-backswing position from where it can be swung *down* to the ball; and (b) to give the arms room to do that swinging. Attempting to "marry" the arm-and-club swing plane too closely to the shoulder-turn plane tends to create excess body action, which inhibits the arm swing and thus reduces clubhead speed.

The *direction* of the swing, the second golf angle created by the backswing, is much simpler to grasp. At the top of any golfer's backswing, the club shaft can be pointing in only one of three directions: parallel to the target line, to the left of it, or to the right of it. By swinging the club up with your hands and arms so that, at the top, the shaft parallels your target line, you put it in the ideal position from which to swing down and through the ball along that line at impact.

Even to the least scientif-ically-minded golfer, it will be evident that the game is likely to become simpler and easier the closer he can get to swinging the club on a sound plane and in the correct direction. Good golf is possible with con-siderable divergence from both these angles, as men like Doug Sanders and Miller Barber prove. But, unless one is physically committed to unusual tendencies, it will be com-plicated golf, necessitating some form of counter-balancing compensation if the club is to be returned along a path that will hit the ball *directly forward*. No one will ever swing perfectly on the right plane and in the right direction all the time

45

For power and position, turn your shoulders 'flatter' than you swing your arms

It is a common misconception, even among good golfers, that the shoulders and arms should move on the same plane in the backswing. Look towards the target from behind any top golfer making a full shot to prove to yourself that this doesn't happen. If the arms are to position the club correctly in the backswing, and swing freely in the through-swing, they must swing *up* as the shoulders turn *around*. Trying to marry your arms to your shoulders introduces too much body action into the shot, at the expense of clubhead speed.

You 'aim' the clubhead at the top as well as at address

If your clubshaft parallels your target line at the top of the backswing, the club is ideally "aimed" to swing back through the ball along the target line. If your shaft is angled left of the target line at the top, there will be a tendency to swing the club-head across the line from out to in and either slice or pull the shot. Conversely, if the shaft is angled right of the target line at the top, there will be a tendency to swing the clubhead from in to out across the target line and either hook or push the shot.

— man not being a machine — but every golfer is likely to benefit from *trying* to do so. This is especially true of the poor player. And in helping him to think more of these important angles than of the usual backswing cliches, I want again to clear up a very common misconception about another aspect of the golf swing's "shape."

An amazing number of people, I have discovered through my teaching over the years, believe that to hit a golf ball straight the club has to be swung from "inside" to "outside" the target line — that at the moment of impact it must be traveling, as it were, from left to right of the target line if you were looking down that line. This idea has been advanced in some illustriously-authored instruction books, and seems to be promulgated by many golf teachers.

It is nonsense. To imagine this yourself, picture a club being swung beneath a sheet of glass inclined at say 45 degrees. It is obvious that, as the club went back, it must, because of the inclination of the glass, travel "inside" a line drawn through the ball to the target. There is no other way it could go, without breaking the glass. Now, picture what would happen during the through-swing. Still touching the glass, the club would come down

again "inside" the target line. At impact, which would happen *on* the target line, the clubhead for a fleeting moment would be going straight along that line. But then what would happen to it? Quite obviously, its path after impact would have to be gradually "inside" again. If it were forced outside, or even continued to go "straight through," it would shatter the glass.

The fact is that an "inside-out" hit will *not* produce a straight shot. If the clubface is open to the target line at impact, the ball will be pushed off to the right, and if the clubface is square or closed, the shot will be drawn or hooked. What produces a straight shot is the clubhead momentarily traveling straight along the target line at impact, on its way from "inside" to "inside," with the clubface square — *and nothing else, whatever you may have read, heard, or believed to have seen.*

Summarizing, let me ask you simply to remember that:

1. You do not hit from "inside to out" if you want a straight shot, only if you are attempting a draw or hook. A straight shot is produced by an "inside-straight-through-inside" swing path.

2. If the club were moving "straight" on the target line all the time, i.e., on a near-vertical plane, the angle of attack on the ball would be too steep, often

producing a feeble, downward blow of little use in propelling the ball forward.

3. If you get all the three dimensions involved at impact right — remember, they are the direction in which the clubhead is traveling, the alignment of its face relative to the target, and the angle of its approach to the ball — *you are bound to hit a good shot.*

How to start back 'square'

A lot of rubbish has been talked and written about the way a golfer should swing the club back from the ball. There have been those who advocated rolling the wrists, those who advocated holding the clubface "square" as long as possible, and those who swore by hooding the clubface during the takeaway.

The "squares" are the ones on the ball, but the trouble is that they don't always define what is truly "square." The golf swing combines an arc and a plane. How, then, do you get "square"?

The answer is by swinging the club away from the ball in one co-ordinated movement — without any **independent** action of any part of the body, especially the hands and arms.

Prove it for yourself as follows. Take your aim and set up correctly for a full shot. Now, without rotating your hands and arms or consciously cocking your wrists, but making the club as near as possible an extension of your left arm, turn and tilt your shoulders slightly and let your arms swing back in concert with this movement. The club will have moved back **inside** the target line — there is no other place it can go if you have set-up and turned properly. And the clubface — where will it point? Not at the sky — which would have happened if you had rolled your wrists clockwise. Not at the ground — which would have happened if you'd held the face down or hooded. It will be pointing more or less **forward** — at right angles to the arc of your swing.

This is "square," as you can very quickly prove by turning your shoulders back to their original position, when the clubface will return squarely behind the ball.

And that is the correct takeaway.

If you build a sound backswing...

So now you're 90 per cent along the way to striking the ball well (grip and set-up); know pretty much what "shape" your swing should have; and understand the geometry of a "square"

Start back like this

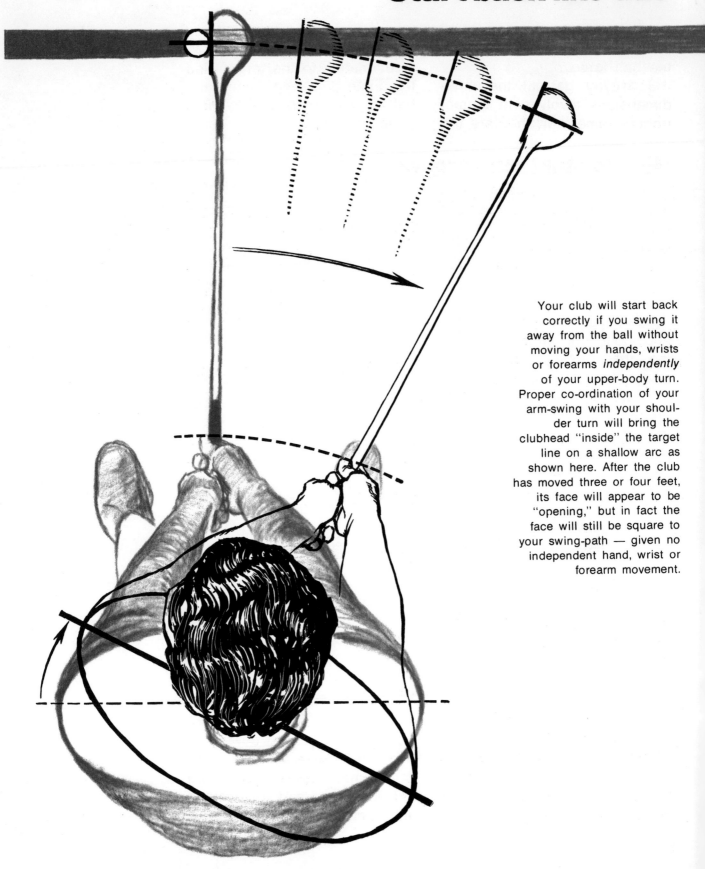

Your club will start back correctly if you swing it away from the ball without moving your hands, wrists or forearms *independently* of your upper-body turn. Proper co-ordination of your arm-swing with your shoulder turn will bring the clubhead "inside" the target line on a shallow arc as shown here. After the club has moved three or four feet, its face will appear to be "opening," but in fact the face will still be square to your swing-path — given no independent hand, wrist or forearm movement.

takeaway. Start the club back correctly and you are 95 per cent of the way. Unfortunately, it is in the first split second of **action** that many players meet their biggest crossroads. One way lies success; the others lead at best to erratic and frustrating golf.

The takeaway is vital because this initial movement of the club largely controls what follows. Not only is the "shape" of the swing cemented by the takeaway, but its overall rhythm is established by the tempo of your starting movement.

The conscious awareness of what initiates the backswing will vary even with the greatest players from day to day. Sometimes it will seem that the hands and arms start the clubhead back. At other times there may be a feeling that the turn of the left shoulder is triggering the swing. Many good golf swings start with a forward press, a slight movement of the hands and hips to the left from which the player "rebounds," so to speak, into a running start. Good golfers rarely start back from complete immobility; in fact, they exhibit a whole variety of little "trigger" movements to keep their action smooth and balanced. The forward press is perhaps the commonest device for starting the club away smoothly and easily. So often the golfer lacking one brings in quick independent wrist action

into his earliest movement.

Whatever the triggering device, a good takeaway produces three effects:

1. Smoothness, rhythm, pace — no snatch or jerk.

2. A coordinated movement ("one-piece," a lot of teachers like to call it), in which the various parts of the body act in unison to maintain both the arc and plane in which the club was set-up at address — no sudden independent, un-coordinated movement of hands, wrists, arms, feet, knees, legs, hips or shoulders.

3. Maintenance, through the first few feet of the swing, of the basic posture and balance established by the set-up, especially a still head and flexed knees — no sudden lifting up, straightening of the legs, swaying of the hips, twisting of the hands, or releasing of the feet from the ground.

If the hands and arms are the transmission of the swing, in that they transmit power to the clubhead, then the source of that power, the engine, is body action. And the fuel for the engine is torque, the turning of the body around the axis of the spine under a steady head. The backswing puts the club into a position from which it can be swung squarely and powerfully into the back of the ball.

I like to compare body action in the golf swing to the winding and unwinding of a spring.

If you wind yourself like a spring...

Your arms and hands transmit power to your clubhead, but your engine is your big body muscles. Their fuel is torque — a spring-like wind-up of your upper body against the resistance of your lower body, around an axis secured by firmly-planted feet and a steady head.

Think of it this way and you will realize how important it is that the bottom half of the "spring" should resist the turning of the top half, in order to increase coiling (and thereby power). In purely golfing terms, this means simply: (1) head steady; (2) feet and legs firmly planted.

Now, "head steady" — rather than "head down" — is one of golf's oldest mandates and it still makes good sense for the majority, so long as it isn't too rigidly applied. If a player can keep his head still **easily** during the swing, he will usually benefit by doing so. His axis will remain constant, and he will not have to make compensations to offset lateral movement. But if a golfer finds it physically difficult to maintain such immobility, he may find it possible to play well with a slight counter-clockwise movement of his head to the right (as many leading players do just before they swing). The real danger is in overdoing any such movement.

A good pivot is usually described as a 90-degree shoulder-turn and a 45-degree hip turn. Unfortunately, achieving this is not easy for many people. It involves considerable use of a lot of muscles, builds up a lot of muscular tension, and it can hurt the untrained golfer enough to prevent him from continually repeating the effort. When that happens, he will take one of two alternatives. Either he will let his hips turn along with — and probably as fully as — his shoulders, or he will turn neither his shoulders nor his hips and simply lift the club up with his hands and arms. Neither produces a powerful swing. The first results in a spin and fling; the second in a lift and a chop.

It must be accepted that learning to make a good upper body turn (in concert with a free arm swing) is a muscular as well as a mental exercise. It demands not only application, but a considerable amount of muscular effort and willpower, especially for the poor player.

One essential in "coiling the spring" is a flexed right knee throughout the backswing and into the downswing. Many golfers find concentrating on keeping the right knee flexed while turning the shoulders fully a short cut to a strong wind-up. Certainly a flexed right knee will cut down hip turn — will stop the tendency to spin the whole body around. More than that, however, it will set up a correct unwind of the hips into the downswing, in a way that keeps the clubhead moving on the correct path through the ball.

One of the main problems faced by the unskilled golfer attempting to master the correct upper body turn is a tendency to "release" with his legs and feet, especially at the start of the backswing. He must consci-

...automatically you will let it all fly

Create sufficient torque with your upper-body backswing wind-up and you cannot help but release it into a powerful through-swing. As your legs and hips win the battle of the opposing forces, and pull springily towards the target, swing your arms straight down before your shoulders spin. Never do anything that will inhibit a free arm-swing.

entiously practice retaining his lower-body set-up position during the first half of the backswing, without collapsing his legs or lifting his left heel way off the ground.

The feeling should be one of staying relatively still but "lively" from the waist down, while your torso turns around the axis of your spine and your arms and hands swing the club back and up so that it ultimately points parallel to the target line. The left leg will give a little, turning in towards the right, and the left heel will usually be pulled rather than lifted off the ground. But the effort should be to prevent, rather than encourage, such movements — **while making sure your shoulders turn as your arms swing the club back and up.**

...your through-swing will be a reflex action

There's a simple way of knowing whether you are coiling properly during your backswing. Try to hold your top-of-the-swing position for 10 seconds. If you've really coiled the spring, you'll find this, if not impossible, certainly a considerable muscular strain.

You will also find that the need to "unwind" is a **reflex** action. As your shoulders reach the limit of their turn, the opposing force in your resisting legs and hips will already be winning the battle. Almost before your shoulders have reached the limit of their turn in one direction, the lower half of your body will have started to pull in the opposite direction. This is what is meant by "starting the downswing with the legs and hips," a recommendation made by nearly every golf book author and modern teacher of the game.

This natural reflex action, the result of opposing forces acting upon each other irresistibly, is the start of the downswing.

It is an observable fact that in a good golf swing, the downswing begins before the backswing finishes. This change of direction, this victory of one force over an opposing force, is, for most golfers, a crossroads equal in magnitude to starting the club away from the ball. The clash of opposing forces **must** take place if the golfer is to get his maximum power into the shot. But it can only take place if he has wound up properly in the backswing. In the backswing the top half of the body has been turning, the lower half resisting, as the arms swing up. In the downswing **the lower half turns while the top half resists and the arms swing down.**

As the lower half of the body wins the battle, the bulk of the player's weight shifts to his left foot while his head stays behind the ball. The legs move laterally to the left and the hips begin to turn to face the hole, thereby clearing the way for the arms to swing the club **down and through** the ball. The right knee — which has been flexed throughout — "kicks in" as the left hip pulls the weight back to the left side. The right leg, now "released," adds thrust to the pull of the left side.

As I've stressed, all of this — subject to a proper wind-up — is largely a reflex action. You can hardly prevent it from happening if you've coiled properly. But the real trick is not in the lower-body action. It lies in the action of the top half, the torso and the head.

Throughout the downswing the head must remain **back;** pretty much where it was at address and during the back-swing, behind the ball. And the upper torso, notably the shoulders, must **resist** the pull of the lower half of the body until the arms have swung down. This is the key to power, the **natural cause** of the "late hit," which so many club golfers have sought so long in vain.

If your top half effectively reverses its backswing role (after resisting the pull and turn of the lower half), the arms and hands, instead of flinging the club from the top — altering the swing's arc and plane, and dissipating power — will be pulled down **inside** the target line. The set or cock of the wrists established by the weight of the club at the top of the swing will be retained until — as the big muscles of the legs, hips and back pull the hands down — the wrists automatically uncock, whipping the clubhead into the ball as the hands flash past it.

These are all the "mechanics" of the through-swing you ever need to know — and ideally you should not even think consciously of them, except in practice sessions. Now let's look at the **coordination** of the actions involved — the vital matter of "timing".

'Timing'—or coordinating clubhead and body action

Timing is a common word in the lexicon of golf. It obviously relates to coordinating all the movements that comprise the swing, but let's give it a more specific meaning?

If a friend said, "Please help me to time my shots better," or, "Show me how to coordinate my swing," would you know what to do, or even where to start? Few golfers would. The word "timing" may convey something to them, but the

'Timing'

Body too far ahead leaves clubface behind hands and thus open to swing-path; swing-path out-to-in across target line; club approaches ball too steeply. Results: whiffing, slicing, topping.

Body "blocking" hands and arms, causing wrists to roll, closing clubface; swing-path in-to-out across target line; club approaches ball too shallowly. Results: hooking, sclaffing, smothering.

Body clearing path for arms to swing clubhead along target line; hands deliver clubface square to swing-path and target line; club approaches ball at correct level to make solid contact. Result: straight, powerful shots.

message is usually fuzzy. It's like that other word often used among golfers, "feel." Everybody must have it, but few can tell other people exactly what it is or how to get it.

Yet it *is* possible to define "timing" and "coordination" in relation to the golf swing. I do so daily in my teaching, and am gratified by the marked improvements that result. Timing is not just a loose, abstract term, signifying something that a golfer either has or does not have, finds or loses, depending on the state of his liver or his bank balance. Timing is related to specific physical components of the golf swing, and it can be adjusted by any player at any time, according to the way he is hitting the ball.

We have seen that the swing is, in fact, a combination of two distinct motive forces and patterns of physical movement. One force is body action, and by "body" I mean the whole of the upper torso, plus the hips, legs and feet. This unit generates power by coiling and uncoiling. Maintaining a fixed axis (by keeping your head steady and anchoring your feet) you coil to the right on the backswing, then uncoil to the left on the downswing.

The other unit of motive force is what most people simply call "hand action," but which I prefer to call arm, wrist and hand action. Working as a swinging

unit, the arms, wrists and hands supply some power to the shot, although their main function is to transmit to the clubhead the much greater power generated by the winding and unwinding of the body.

If you can grasp this simple concept of the golf swing, you should have no difficulty in understanding what timing is all about. In fact, probably without my spelling it out, you will have suspected that a perfectly coordinated or timed golf swing is one in which the coiling and uncoiling actions of the body mate perfectly with the swinging action of the arm, wrist and hands unit — **to deliver the clubface squarely to the ball with maximum speed at the moment of impact.**

Lack of arm-wrist-hand action, combined with too much body action, is what causes so many club golfers to suffer from such erratic swing coordination. They try to play like the pros with only half the muscular equipment. Lacking a top golfer's natural clubhead speed, they try to make up for it by copying his body action. The result is invariably a hectic imbalance of physical movement and muscular effort, which destroys their timing.

When I explain this to golfers on the driving range, some of them assume that what I am really saying is that they will never play well because they aren't strong or healthy enough. This is not the case at all. Most reasonably fit people possess, and can transmit to the club-head, enough speed with their arms and hands to hit decent golf shots, without playing seven days a week or under-going special exercise — **so long as they will learn to swing the clubhead into the ball,** in-stead of throwing their bodies at it. But more on that later.

Once you understand how the body pivot and the arm-and-hand swing inter-relate, it is easy to diagnose and correct poor swing coordination for yourself. The way your shots fly tells you whether the two are in balance or not.

Let's assume that your playing methods are basically sound. You use a grip that nor-mally returns the clubface correctly. You aim the clubface and yourself properly. There is nothing seriously wrong with the shape of your swing. You should, therefore, hit straight and solid shots. But you are not. You are slicing a lot of shots, and topping or thinning others.

When this happens the fault is almost always poor co-ordination. You are using too much body action in the down-swing, relative to your arm and hand action. The fault most probably occurs at the moment you transfer from the backswing into the downswing. It is caused by uncoiling your body too fast,

jerkily, or violently, in relation to your arm-hand-clubhead swing. The effect of this excessive un-wind of the body is to delay your arm and hand swing so that the clubface arrives open at im-pact — pointing right of target — and on so steep a plane that it hits only the upper portion of the ball. In other words, you have hit **too late** with your arms, wrists, hands and clubhead, and **too early** with your body. Your body uncoil has dragged your arms, wrists and hands past and over the ball before you could square the clubface and swing it solidly into the back of the ball.

If you are slicing or topping shots, simply slow down your lower body unwind and in-crease the use of the clubhead by speeding up your arm-swing. Hit **earlier** with the clubhead and **later** with the body, until the flight of the ball tells you that you have struck a balance. Think predominantly of swing-ing the clubhead **down and through the ball with arms before your shoulders unwind.**

If you have the other problem, if you are hooking the ball or hitting shots fat, you need the opposite treatment. Your coor-dinative problem is simply that your arm and hand swing is ahead of your body unwind. This is a timing affliction that of-ten troubles the good golfer. He is so eager to whip the club-head into the ball that he

63

Why women golfers raise up on their toes

Few women golfers have the physical strength that enables good men players to delay the "release" of the clubhead until late in the downswing. Many women who attempt to "hit late" by holding back the clubhead with their wrists actually reduce their distance because this effort causes them to mis-hit the ball. Thus most women golfers would hit the ball farther by straightening their right arm sooner in the downswing. It is to allow clearance for this "earlier" arm swing hit and wider downswing arc that many good women golfers rise onto their toes just before and during impact.

doesn't properly initiate the downswing with an uncoiling to the left of his legs and hips. And, because his hips haven't cleared a passage, there is no room for his fast-moving arms to swing past his body and out towards the target as they should. Instead, he is forced to roll his wrists, closing the club-face so that it faces left of target at impact.

Again the cure is simple. Just speed up your leg and hip action relative to the movement of your arm, wrist and hand unit. You must be sure to initiate the downswing by turning your left hip to the left and keeping it going, at the same time delay-ing your arm and hand swing. Very soon, solidly-struck straight shots will indicate that you have found the correct balance.

A lot has been written in recent years about playing golf with a "body" method, and this has been answered by exponents of a "hands" method. As I see it, there has never been enough accent on **arms.** If the arms work, so will the wrists and hands — and thus the clubhead. But the good golf swing is neither primarily "body action" nor primarily "clubhead action": it is **a perfect blend or balance of both.** And the word for that is "timing."

Ladies, you CAN hit it farther!

With very few exceptions, women do not hit the ball as far as they could. Indeed, the long hitter among women is immediately exceptional, and will often come into national and even international prominence as a golfer almost on the strength of this ability alone. Such is not true of men's golf, where achieving distance is much less a problem than controlling it.

It is true, of course, that women do not hit the ball so far as men because they do not have the physical equipment to generate comparable clubhead speed. What the woman player must realize, however, is that distance isn't just clubhead speed — it is clubhead speed **accurately applied.** While maybe limited to the extent she can increase her actual clubhead speed, there is usually a great deal she can do to deliver what she possesses more effectively to the ball. It is, in fact, incorrect application of the club — not lack of strength — that makes so many ladies play what I describe as pat-ball golf.

The same clubhead speed that many women golfers apply down and across the ball, with the clubface open, would hit it a heck of a lot farther if it were applied with the clubhead traveling virtually parallel to the

*ground and along the target line
with the face square.*

Where distance is concerned,
it is paramount for the club to
approach the ball from **directly
behind**, as opposed to from
above and behind. To swing the
clubhead into the very back of
the ball on a shallow arc in the
impact zone, a woman must use
her arms, wrists and hands
earlier in the downswing than
does a man. For most women
golfers, this means a conscious,
deliberate effort to get their
arms really going from the top
of the backswing. There are two
reasons for this: (1) it takes
longer for a woman to reach her
maximum clubhead speed; and
(2) the clubhead is more likely
to approach the ball from directly behind, rather than from
above, and thus achieve flush
contact.

Effects of "hitting earlier" are
very noticeable in the swings of
top woman golfers, and any
club player anxious to improve
would do well to study them.
She will see that a great many
good women players come up
on their toes during the downswing and remain there until
well after impact — Lady Heath-
coat-Amory (Joyce Wethered)
was a classic example of this
type of action. The reason for it,
of course, is to allow the
clubhead to swing squarely into
the ball on the shallow-bot-
tomed arc engendered by an
earlier hit, without it touching

the ground behind the ball.

Another result of hitting earlier among ladies is an absence
of "dinner-plate" divots with the
irons. Few women have the
muscular strength to hit down
and through on a steep arc with
an iron. Hitting earlier brings
the clubhead into the ball on a
flatter trajectory, with less
divot — but produces just as effective a shot, so long as the
ball isn't "scooped."

How does a woman golfer hit
"earlier?"

First, she determines that, for
evermore, she will not be content to play pat-ball, but will
really try to **swish** the club
through the ball as fast as possible. This is the mental hurdle
that most women club golfers
(and a few of better standard)
must first surmount if they are
going to improve substantially.

On the physical side, the first
major factor for attention is
usually the grip. Most women
tend to cut the ball, and, if this
is the case, they must not be
frightened of adopting a powerful grip. The left hand particularly should be placed well
on top of the shaft, with up to
three knuckles showing and the
thumb well to the right side of
the grip. The shaft should be
held firmly in both the palm and
fingers, and there should be a
feeling that the club is nestling
deep into the hand so that the
fingers can really hold onto it (if
this isn't possible the grips are

too thick). The right hand may need to be a little under the shaft, the "V" of thumb and forefinger pointing between the right ear and right shoulder, with the club held snug in the fingers, and the forefinger "triggered" around the shaft.

The grip should feel firm, yet leave the arms flexible, not tense or rigid. If this is difficult with the overlapping grip, try an interlocking or double-handed grip (ensuring, of course, that your hands are as close together as possible). Some experiment may be necessary, expecially if you have tended to hold the club "weakly" — left hand well to the left and right hand on top. Don't be frightened to make it.

A woman who cuts the ball should never stand to her shots in an "open" position — with feet, hips and shoulders aimed left of the target. A slightly closed shoulder alignment will not only help her to swing the club solidly into the back of the ball, but will encourage an inside-out angle of attack that will produce a touch of distance-generating "draw."

A wide arc on the backswing is even more essential to women golfers than it is to men, simply to make room for the bigger arc on the way down that is imperative if they are to get the clubhead really motoring. Indeed, most women golfers sense this need for a wide backswing, but unfortunately their efforts to achieve it often lead to loss of control, through excessive body movement or a tendency to sway.

Women find it difficult to coil their bodies; to "wind the spring" that puts power into a golf shot. In an effort to get the necessary width of arc, they release from the ground, turn their whole torso from the feet, as the initial backswing movement. Women as well as men must learn to keep the head reasonably still to "anchor" the swing; and to turn the upper body from the hips up, while the feet and legs resist.

I am often taken to task for advising players, men and women, to hit earlier with the clubhead, but it is a fact that only when the swing lacks a correct wind-up does early use of the clubhead lead to trouble. Without lower-body resistance, an early hit means a feeble pass at the ball with only the arms and hands. When the swing is correctly anchored and there is a good wind-up of the upper body, a strong swing down of the arms and clubhead is essential to keep pace with the reflex release and uncoiling of the legs and hips.

FUNDAMENTALS OF SWING MOVEMENT

Every star swings FLUIDLY

It is said that no two golf swings are alike. Indeed, this argument is often used against the numerous "methods" or set patterns of swinging, which, by the score, have fashionably contorted golfers down the years. The argument is, of course, valid. No two golf swings are alike, because no two individuals are alike.

Nevertheless, it will be obvious to anyone who has studied the golf swing that, however wide the variations in the overall actions of good golfers, each contains common fundamentals.

It is these fundamentals above all that the lesser golfer must strive to acquire if he is to benefit from any study of superior players. Unfortunately, to do so is difficult. The good golf swing is such a fast and fluid movement that, in watching golfers, or in looking at pictures of the golf action when "stopped," the eye tends to hit upon peculiarities or idiosyncrasies rather than fundamentals. These images are then transmitted to the brain, which instinctively tries to correlate them with earlier impressions and existing information. All too often the result is distortion. That is why I always concern myself with fundamentals, and why in this section I want to talk about the "fundamentals of movement."

Put together and coordinated, they are to be found in the actions of the majority of the world's top golfers.

Whatever your 'method,' your arms must SWING

Why arms to start? "Surely," I can imagine readers saying, "the golf swing starts in the hands, or the feet, or the left shoulder."

Undoubtedly it does, for various players at various times, depending on how they are swinging and how they are adjusting to stay in their own particular groove. But we are not concerned now with starts or middles or stops. We are concerned primarily with ac-tions — fundamental actions. And the fundamental action in the golf swing is without a shadow of doubt the swinging of the arms. If you are to play well, you must swing them *freely*.

"Yes, of course," you say. "And I do." I would suggest, sir and madam, if your handicap is between 36 and 12, that you do *not*. You may **think** you make a free arm swing, but my experience tells me that somewhere in

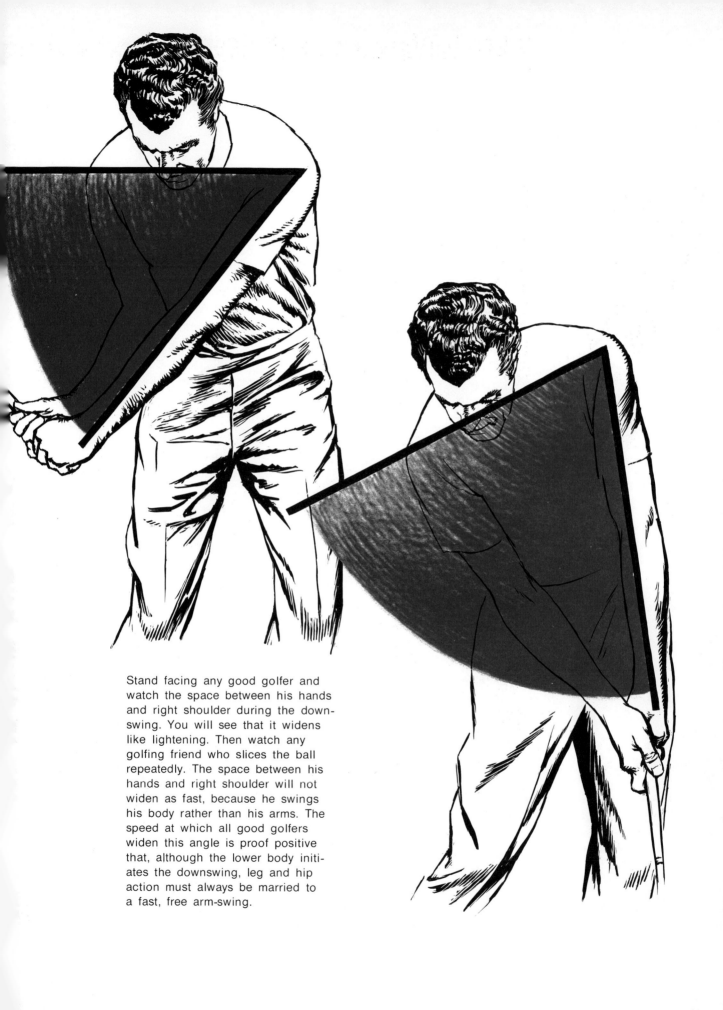

Stand facing any good golfer and watch the space between his hands and right shoulder during the downswing. You will see that it widens like lightening. Then watch any golfing friend who slices the ball repeatedly. The space between his hands and right shoulder will not widen as fast, because he swings his body rather than his arms. The speed at which all good golfers widen this angle is proof positive that, although the lower body initiates the downswing, leg and hip action must always be married to a fast, free arm-swing.

your swing, if you have not yet progressed to the limit of your natural golfing ability (which is far higher than most players will believe), something is interfering with the free, fast flailing which should and could be your arm action.

The arm action in golf has had surprisingly little attention. Millions of words have been written about hands, shoulders, hips, feet, but hardly a thought seems to have been given to the arms as such.

I think this is chiefly because the arms in golf are confused with the hands. Indeed, in much teaching, "hands" is used as a synonym for "arms." "Swing the club (or the clubhead) with the hands" is an adage almost as old as the game itself, and still sums up probably the most widely accredited "method" today. Yet, if you think about it, you soon realize that the hands themselves **cannot** swing the club. All they can do is hold on while the arms swing it.

It seems to me that how the hands work is determined not by any involuntary or independent action of these extremities themselves, but by the movement of the arms. And the movement of the arms — their free, fast, flailing action on the correct plane — is, let me say again, an absolute fundamental of good golf. In this movement lies the difference between the 250-yard drive of the star golfer

and the puny efforts of many middle- and high-handicap players.

The reason why the arms must swing free is quite simple. When they do we are able to apply the clubhead to the ball at our maximum speed. When they do not, we are generally forced to apply **ourselves** to the ball; the flail of the arms is replaced by a heave of the shoulders. And it is this shoulder heave, this hurling of the torso into the shot, that limits so many golfers who, potentially, could possess a single-figure handicap.

Henry Cotton says "use the hands" — that therein lies the key to golf. I would agree with him 100 per cent if he said "use the hands and arms." It seems to me that if the arms don't work, the hands are virtually helpless, whereas if the arms swing freely both the wrists and hands can and will work to their fullest. Indeed, anyone who has the facility to make a full, free arm swing and a reasonable body turn has, in my experience, all the physical equipment necessary to play excellent golf. Conversely, no matter how orthodox a player's "pattern of movements" may be, without a free arm swing he will rarely achieve a satisfying level of skill.

How does one acquire a good arm swing? We will go into that in a moment, but before doing so let me give you the simple exercise that I have found helps more than any other to promote the feel of a good arm swing. **This drill is to hit balls with your feet absolutely together. In this position it is virtually impossible to make a shot other than with a free swinging of the arms, hands and clubhead, because any excessive use of the body leads to complete loss of balance.** I find that I can hit the ball within 20 yards of my normal distance with my feet together, and I would recommend this exercise for any golfer who tends to slice or top many shots.

Getting to the specifics of how the arms should work, the first thing to be understood is that the arm swing is closely allied to the shoulder wind-up in the backswing, and to the hip unwind in the downswing. Two pieces of geometry are involved in the backswing. First, the arms must swing **in harmony with the shoulders** as they turn. Secondly, the shoulders must turn a full 90 degrees.

If the shoulders turn only 60 degrees in the backswing, a free arm-swing on the way down is likely to bring the club across the target line from out to in. Conversely, a 120-degree turn (much rarer) would tend to make the arms swing the club across the ball from inside-to-outside the line. Assuming that the arms work in close harness with the shoulders, a turn pretty close to 90 degrees sets up the geometry for them to swing the clubhead freely into the ball while it is moving along the target line.

Many average golfers, and even some good ones, do not make a correct shoulder turn, yet they frequently swing the club into the ball more or less along the right path. They do so by compensating, by making some corrective movement either at the start of, or during, the downswing.

Consequently, the pre-requisite of good arm action is a full wind-up of the shoulders on the backswing. To describe this movement I could use the term "one-piece," but I don't want to because I think it has been overdone. Anyone who over-deliberately tries to take the clubhead away "in one piece," as a start-back feeling, is certainly going to stop his arms swinging freely. The movement is not a "take." It's a swing. What "one-piece" really means is "nothing working independently" — a correlated movement away from the ball in which the shoulders turn smooth and the arms swing freely.

Always let your arms, hands and club swing back, folding the right arm naturally and easily as the movement requires, keeping the left arm fairly straight. (Straight, not stiff; a stiff left arm will inhibit your golf game much more than a bent one.)

SWEEP those arms down and through

The action of the arms is the most neglected area in golf instruction. There have been "hands" methods, and "body" methods, but the fact is that, whatever method he hung his hat on, every good golfer in history has swept the club through the ball fast and freely with his arms.

Try, above all, to avoid the two commonest faults in the backswing movement: (1) picking up the club by lifting the shoulders, which disturbs your swing plane; (2) using independent hand action either to roll the clubface open or hold it down and shut by trying forcefully to keep it "square." Concentrate instead on making a **swing** of your arms the initial movement of the backswing. If you find this difficult, do it as a rebound action off a slight forward press.

Don't worry about your wrists. I can assure you that, if your right arm folds properly — and many followers of so-called "square" methods delay this folding too long — and your left arm remains reasonably straight, your wrists will hinge automatically. (It might be worth mentioning here, for clarification, that in the normal golf swing there is no such thing as a deliberate wrist cock. The wrists cock and uncock purely as a result of centrifugal force created by the weight of the clubhead and the swinging of the arms. Doing things deliberately with your wrists is a sure way to founder your game. I might also add that wrist action is a tremendous variable over which every man is a law unto himself.)

Coming now to the downswing, two of the commonest faults in golf prevent the arms from really working, moving, *swinging.* One is prematurely turning or spinning the shoulders into the shot — a "shoulder heave," a throwing of the body into the action; an application of the player to the ball instead of the clubhead. The other fault is prematurely uncocking the wrists — the release of power long before the clubhead is in position to strike the ball squarely. This jerky attempt to force clubhead to ball with the hands from the top of the swing often results from a misdirected effort to increase clubhead speed with "hand action," instead of a fast, free swinging of the arms.

There are two ways of "hitting from the top." One is too-early an application of the shoulders and upper body. The other is too early a release of the power stored in the wrists, forced as they are into a cocked position by the weight of the clubhead. **Both result, nine times out of ten, from insufficient or "late" arm swing on the way down.** Any player suffering from lack of power or poor balance should have one simple thought at the top of his backswing: to start down with his arms, to make **his arms swing the clubhead down and through the ball.**

It is, of course, a fact that the good player's downswing is started and led by the legs and hips (and this has become a fundamental of teaching). But, believe me, it is no good for the player who lacks a free arm swing to think of starting his downswing with his legs or hips. Doing so will simply lead to an early unwinding — a heaving "out and over" — of his shoulders.

To my way of thinking, almost every movement in the golf swing is subject to a full, free arm swing, but the fact has rarely been emphasized, for the simple reason that the good players who write books on golf usually make the erroneous assumption that, like themselves, their readers have both strong hands and free-swinging arms.

It will be obvious that the critical word in all of the foregoing is **swing.** I cannot over-stress its importance. But, to try to get this message into a nutshell, let me say this: If you can turn your shoulders and swing a straight (but not stiff) left arm in the backswing, then unwind your hips while swinging your arms freely in the downswing, you won't be far from a very good golf game. If you can then add the feeling of hitting **through** the ball on an extended right arm, you'll be very close to an exceptional golf game.

The legs lead the through-swing

It is widely recognized that good leg action is essential to good golf. Unfortunately, few average players really understand what constitutes good leg action. In fact, there is probably as much confusion about this department of the swing as about any technical aspect of the game.

Thus it might be as well to start by trying to correct what seems to be the most general misconception about the task of the legs in the golf swing. Most golfers know that they must work, so many make a deliberate, conscious effort to get them to do so. This usually leads to trouble. It is, for instance, the main cause of the "ballet dancing" that is so common a spectacle on golf courses around the world every weekend.

If you study the great players in action, and compare their movements with the swings of your friends, you will find that in most cases the good players, on the backswing, have considerably *less* movement from the waist down than do club golfers, but considerably *more* in the through-swing. This is a direct result of resistance, torque, spring-like coiling. The good player coils in the backswing against the resistance of his feet and legs. The release of this power in the through-swing results in strong, positive movements from the waist down

Leg resistance on backswing triggers proper reaction on through-swing

On the backswing your feet and legs should resist the coiling action of your upper body. If they do so properly, they will trigger your downswing as a *reflex* uncoiling action. So set-up to the ball with your feet planted, your knees flexed and feeling "springy" from the waist down.

as the spring "springs." The poor player fails to supply the necessary resistance in his legs and feet. He dances around in such a way that there can be no build-up of torque, no coiling of the spring, in the backswing. Then, there being nothing to release in the through-swing, he is either stiff and wooden in his legs or collapses completely when he comes to hit the ball.

The golf ball cannot be struck powerfully and accurately with any action other than that comparable to the wind-up and release of a coil spring.

If the golfer will believe this, and work at it, he will soon realize that his feet and legs are a critical part of his anatomy. They are his contact with the ground, his platform, and their task is nothing more nor less than to resist — to anchor the end of the spring to a base during both its coiling and release. If that doesn't happen, the result invariably is that the player swings his body rather than the club at the ball — the old story of applying oneself rather than the clubhead.

I think "relax" has been one of the most damaging words in golf teaching, in that it has often been applied to the whole of the set-up, rather than to upper areas of the body, where relaxation can promote freedom of movement. For the majority of players, however, relaxation from the hips down is one of the

worst thoughts to have in mind. Freedom of movement of the feet and legs is exactly what **isn't** required.

In saying this, I realize a need for care. There will be those who read into these words a necessity to root themselves to the ground like telegraph poles. Although for the majority this might be better than ballet dancing, it is not the key to correct foot and leg work. Stiffness is never desirable in **any** aspect of golf.

What we seek, in terms of leg action, is a happy medium between rooted stiffness and uncontrolled sloppiness. Perhaps the best word to describe the feel is "liveliness" — a sensation that we are planted firmly on the floor, but that from this base we can generate and control the power in the spring system overhead.

Perhaps I can put across the feeling by reiterating that, in my concept of the good golf swing, it is impossible to hold a top-of-the-swing position for more than a few seconds, **because the sheer muscular strain on the legs and hips of the correct wind-up will force them to unwind after a very brief period.**

It is often said that the golf swing starts on the ground, and there is no denying this (try swinging sitting in a chair if you want proof). Unfortunately, taking the idea literally, many players tend to initiate the swing with a ground-level movement, generally either by lifting the left heel or collapsing the left knee forward, or both. They are dead ducks from that moment on.

Foot and leg action is never an initiating movement, but is the **result** of the initial movements, which are the swing away of the arms and club and the turn or wind-up of the shoulders.

Thus, a feeling of "liveliness" should always be sought at address. To promote this, for a full swing, your weight should be comfortably balanced between the balls and heels of each foot, but favoring the balls if anything. You should strive for firmness and a sense of balance, but also a feeling that you are ready to take off — a poised sensation similar, perhaps, to that of an athlete preparing to run or jump. Above all, your knees **must** be flexed, and — this is an absolute fundamental — **the right knee must remain flexed throughout the swing.**

If you address the ball, then make the movement that would be your initial movement in sitting down, you are going a long way to establishing the correct set-up for good foot and leg action. But beware that you don't — as so many do — stand up again on a straightened right leg as you begin to swing.

If you start your swing correctly, your left heel will **not** shoot up off the ground; you will **not** spin on your left toe as your whole body wobbles round to the right; your left knee will **not** cave in; your right knee will **not** straighten and lock. The correct start to a lively, springy wind-up will begin to affect the left foot and leg some time after the club has gone back — usually as it reaches about hip height. Around that stage of the swing your left knee will be dragged, by the sheer torque of the wind-up, in towards your right leg. Your left heel may rise slightly, the amount depending on your build and suppleness. But the chief movement of your left foot will be to roll in towards the right, pulling the weight remaining on your left side onto the inside of your left foot, not onto the toe. Throughout this wind-up action, your right leg will hardly move. Above all, your right knee must not straighten.

I might add that in the swings of most top players, the left heel comes off the ground, if it comes off at all, as the **last** action of the backswing, and returns solidly to the ground as the **first** action of the downswing. When a golfer tries deliberately to generate foot action, invariably he reverses this action. Good foot action **follows** in the backswing and **leads** in the downswing.

It might be as well, while we're on the subject of feet and legs, to say something about weight transference — a highly controversial point in golf teaching. Quite candidly, I believe that much of the talk about weight transference has done a lot of harm to a lot of golfers. As I see it, there should **never** be a conscious or deliberate effort to transfer weight one way or the other in the golf swing. Doing so — apart from promoting all sorts of strange dance-like antics — leads to a host of other faults, of which tilting and swaying the entire body are prime examples. If your upper body winds up against the springy resistance of your feet and legs, whatever weight transfer is necessary will occur naturally on your backswing.

The same applies on the downswing. If what has gone before is correct, if your downswing starts with a co-ordinated hip movement and arm-swing, your feet and legs will do their job automatically, and transfer your weight naturally. But if your backswing is wrong, with your left leg releasing and your right leg stiffening, it is virtually impossible for your legs and hips to work correctly on the way down. Instead, your shoulders will be forced to take over in that commonest — and ugliest — of all golfing sights, the collapsing heave.

THE
SHORT
GAME

'See' your shot, THEN choose a club

Mentally picturing how you want the ball to behave is the foundation of a strong short game. Until you decide how the ball must fly and roll, you cannot select the club that will do the job most easily.

Mental pictures must come first

The golfer with an effective short game, the man or woman who can consistently lay those little pitch and chip shots close enough to the hole for a single putt, really does have a tremendous advantage. Confidence in one's short game gives a tremendous edge at all levels of competition.

The sad thing is that so few people command a sound short game when, whatever their standard with the long shots, it is well within their reach. Here is the area of the game where the fellow who booms the ball 300 yards off the tee is pulled back to equal terms with the chap who can never manage more than 170 yards. This is the department of golf that calls for nothing more than good mental imagery and "touch."

The techniques for pitching and chipping are simple, but before getting into them I want to stress this imagery factor. You should never play a short shot until you have a clear mental picture of how you want the ball to behave. This really is the secret of a strong short game. Until you decide how far and high the ball should fly, where it should land and how much it should roll, you cannot select the right club for the job. And what prevents so many people from developing a good short game is their illogical use of the same favorite club for every shot. There is **no way** that one club will get the ball close to the hole in every situation when you miss a green. Yet, even when I am teaching classes of international players, and ask what club they use for chipping, someone says: "I always use a seven-iron."

By using the wrong club for the particular shot at hand, you introduce a needless variable. If you choose a club with too much loft for a little chip from the fringe, in some way you will have to de-loft it during the stroke. Conversely, if you choose a too-straight-faced club, there will be a tendency to scoop at the ball to get it into the air. Selection of the correct club will allow you to play the same, simple stroke under all circumstances, with the club's loft automatically governing flight and roll.

Watch the extreme care with which the pros think out and plan these little shots in tournaments and you will get an idea of how important it is to "picture" the shot, then select the club that will match the picture.

Cause and effect in chipping and pitching

The chip shot is used around the green when there are no hazards between your ball and the hole. The object is to drop the ball on the edge of the putting surface and let it run the rest of the way to the hole. Club selection is governed largely by the distance the ball must carry through the air before reaching the green, and the amount of green between you and the hole. For example, from a few feet off the putting surface a five-iron might loft the ball to the edge of the green, from where it would roll to the hole. But from 15 yards out your ball would roll too far. Thus you'd probably need an eight-iron or an even more-lofted club.

The pitch shot is the exact opposite of the chip. You use a nine-iron, pitching-wedge or sand-wedge to hit the ball high through the air so that it lands and stops as quickly as possible. It is the shot to play over hazards, or when the green is wet and holding, or for some reason the amount of roll is difficult to judge.

The major difference between the two shots is that you are trying to minimize back-spin with a chip shot and to maximize it with a pitch shot. Under normal conditions the chip shot is the safer of the two, because roll is easier to judge than flight, and easier to control. Also, most golfers find it easier on short shots to make solid contact with a less-lofted club, the extreme example being, of course, a putter.

The first step in getting ready to play either a chip or pitch is the same as for any other golf shot. You aim the clubface correctly, take your proper grip on the club, then place your feet in relation to the clubface. On both chip and pitch shots, it helps to have your weight predominantly on the left leg, and to set your hands ahead of the clubface. Your legs should be comfortably flexed and your body fairly relaxed (but never crouched over the ball). Place your feet fairly close together in a slightly open stance, but keep your shoulders parallel to the target line.

Don't fall into the common error of letting your shoulders follow the line of your feet. Although the foot stance can be slightly open, your shoulders should remain parallel to the target line. If the ball is addressed with the shoulders open, you will tend to swing to the left of target, and will be obliged to hold the blade of the club open at impact to hit the ball in the right direction. "Blocking" the shot at impact like this makes it difficult to control distance.

Neither a chip nor a short pitch shot requires conscious body action. All you need is a smooth back-and-through-swing with your arms, hands and club — an unrushed, even-paced movement, in which the clubface never passes the hands until the ball has been

85

Chip with arms, but add wrists to pitch

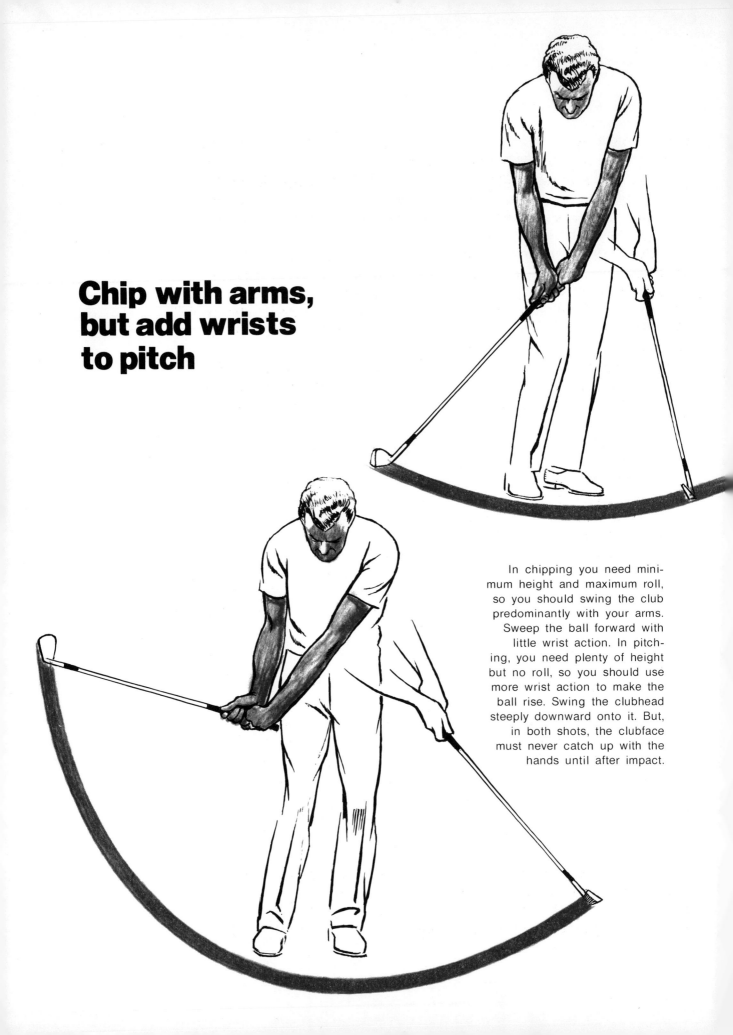

In chipping you need minimum height and maximum roll, so you should swing the club predominantly with your arms. Sweep the ball forward with little wrist action. In pitching, you need plenty of height but no roll, so you should use more wrist action to make the ball rise. Swing the clubhead steeply downward onto it. But, in both shots, the clubface must never catch up with the hands until after impact.

STRIKING
THE BALL

sent on its way.

In both pitching and chipping, the length of shot is determined largely by the length of your backswing. Too short a backswing will lead you to stab quickly at the ball, but swing the club back too far and you'll tend to slow it down before impact. In your mental picture of the shot you will have selected a spot on the green where you want the ball to land. Take a few practice swings until you find the length that you sense will hit the ball to this spot. A few minutes' practice will tell you how far the ball travels through the air for various lengths of backswing.

Because the chip is played when there are no obstacles between you and the hole, the height and flight of the shot is dictated by the loft of the club you select. Thus you need little or no wrist action when chipping. You play pitch shots, however, in a wide variety of situations that call for different degrees of height and distance. For example, if the ball has to be pitched over a bunker with the pin set close to the edge of the green on the near side, a soft lob shot would be required. This involves positioning the ball well forward at address, opening the clubface, and keeping your hands level with the ball at address and impact. On the other hand, if you were playing a longish pitch shot into

the wind, you would need to move the ball back at address, hooding the clubface slightly by keeping your hands well in front of the ball at address and impact.

A steep, downward hit is necessary to pitch effectively, and that requires more wrist action than in the chip-shot stroke. The set-up is very much as for the chip — feet close together, stance slightly open, weight on the left side, and hands ahead of the clubface. But that is as far as the similarity goes. In the pitch-shot backswing, the wrists should cock easily and remain cocked throughout the downswing — your left hand must "lead" the clubface through impact.

Beware of trying to scoop the ball into the air by leaning back on the right foot and hitting upwards with the clubhead. Set your weight on your left foot, keep it there, and hit down into the ball — the loft of the club will get it airborne rapidly.

Many golfers seem to have the erroneous idea that pitching well involves "cutting the ball up" — swinging into the ball from outside the target line and holding or "blocking" the face of the club open at impact. This is a useful shot in certain circumstances, as when the ball must fly high and stop virtually in its own pitch mark, but it is not an easy shot to play and requires considerable confidence.

Stand 'open'...

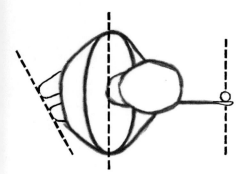

...but not 'across'

Your body does not need to coil and uncoil for a chip or short pitch shot — you swing the club primarily with your hands and arms. But you do need room to swing your arms past your body, and opening your stance — pulling your left foot back a little — helps you clear your left side. The danger is that you may also set your shoulders "open" to the target line by instinctively matching their alignment to your stance. When this happens, in trying to swing the club straight back along your target line you will actually have to pull it "inside" relative to your shoulder alignment. More often than not the result will be a "rebound" that throws the club outside the target line on the through-swing. This is the chief cause of the most common short game fault — pulling the ball left.

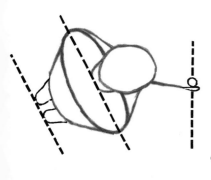

Too many people try to play every pitch shot this way, and thus turn a relatively simple shot into a difficult one. Watch any of the world's great wedge players and you will see that they most frequently "draw" the ball to the pin — moving it slightly from right to left — and yet still make it spin back off the second bounce. They achieve this stopping power much more through backspin — created by a sharp, accurate, downward hit — than by a high trajectory.

The technique for the chip shot is very close to that for the pitch, with one vital difference: whereas the pitch shot requires a free cocking of the wrists in the backswing, the chip shot requires more of an arm swing — although the wrists should never be rigid. Assuming you have a good lie, the chip shot is a firm, controlled **sweep** with the arms and club working as a unit, with just a little "give" in the wrists and hips to prevent the action from being jerky or wooden.

One point I would stress again to sum up concerns the path of the swing. Although the club swings straight back from the ball initially, it soon must move **inside** the target line if we are going to be able to swing it straight through the ball at impact. Since the follow-through is often curtailed on short shots, "inside to straight-through" is a good mental picture for the club's path on chip and pitch shots. If you are a confessed bad short-game player, I am sure "seeing" the stroke this way will help you.

Putting: 'see' the line and STRIKE the ball

Putting is not golf: it is a game within golf. How good you are at hitting the ball through the air bears little relation to how well you can roll it along the ground.

Putting is largely a matter of instinct, "touch" and nerve. The old lady at the seaside playing to amuse her grand-child can be better at it than the world-class professional, playing for a fortune.

Thus if you are naturally a good putter, nothing — and I mean **nothing** — should persuade you to change your method or your approach to this part of the game. If you can get the ball in the hole when it matters, how you do so is of no consequence.

Unfortunately, the better a golfer becomes at the through-the-air game, the more important his putting becomes. If you hit a green 500 yards away in four strokes and get down in one putt, you are pleased. If you hit it in two strokes then take three more to hole out, you are incensed.

Most golfers never totally

evade putting problems. The following is for this unfortunate majority. If you are naturally a good putter, read no farther.

It seems to me that golfers who putt poorly, especially if they miss the short ones, do so above all else because they lack *authority* of stroke. Nervousness, "pressure," lack of confidence, lack of concentration, the general tizz that this game can wrap us in, leads to indecisiveness about line and distance; and, worse still, about striking the ball. We tend to wave at it, coax it, steer it, drag it, jab it, twitch it — anything but **hit** it.

Consequently, the poor putter needs, first, a mental resolution, a determination to strike the ball with the putterhead; and, second, a method that encourages him to do so. The first is a question of total mental commital to a particular line. Sometimes we can "see" the line better than at other times. But, whatever you do, you must commit yourself totally to strike the ball in a certain direction.

The shortest route to an authoritative strike, I believe, is to hit the ball **against** the left wrist, never past it. On short putts the left wrist never quits nor bends at any stage of the forward stroke. There are two easy ways to do this. In one the club is swung with the arms, wrists and hands in one piece — a firm, from-the-shoulders,

pendulum-type action in which there is no independent movement of any part of the unit. In the other the backswing is initiated with a break back of the left wrist (often from a little forward press), but on the through-swing the wrist is not broken forward. It remains hinged back as the through-swing is made, the ball being tapped against the firm, still-hinged wrist joint. In other words, the player "returns" his left wrist but never lets his putter face pass it.

On short putts, the latter style is very common among tournament players in the U.S.A. today. It enables the ball to be struck firmly and crisply with a rapping or tapping action, diminishing the possibility of the clubface rolling shut and pulling the ball left, as can so easily happen if the left wrist "gives" on the through-swing.

Some golfers may interpret what I've just described as a stiff-wristed action. It isn't. There is a wrist-break going back, but none going forward, so that the clubface never gets ahead of the hands until well after impact. The method's biggest danger lies in "blocking" the tapping action of the right hand too much with the left wrist, resulting in a pushed putt.

As we get farther away from the hole, there is a "softening" in this kind of action, of course. The strike becomes more of a

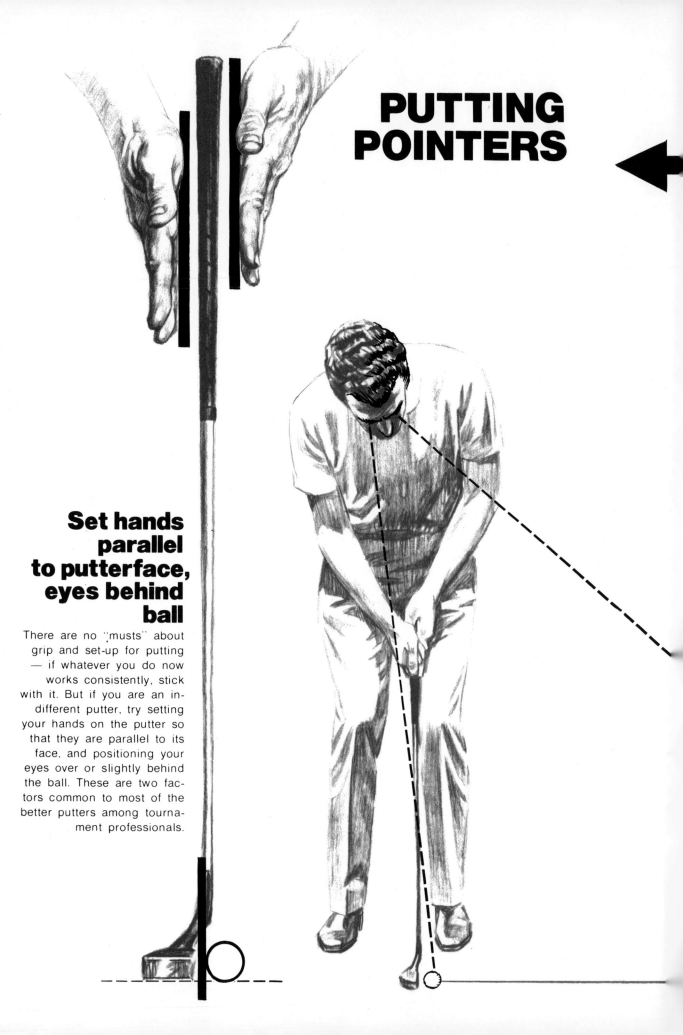

PUTTING POINTERS

Set hands parallel to putterface, eyes behind ball

There are no "musts" about grip and set-up for putting — if whatever you do now works consistently, stick with it. But if you are an indifferent putter, try setting your hands on the putter so that they are parallel to its face, and positioning your eyes over or slightly behind the ball. These are two factors common to most of the better putters among tournament professionals.

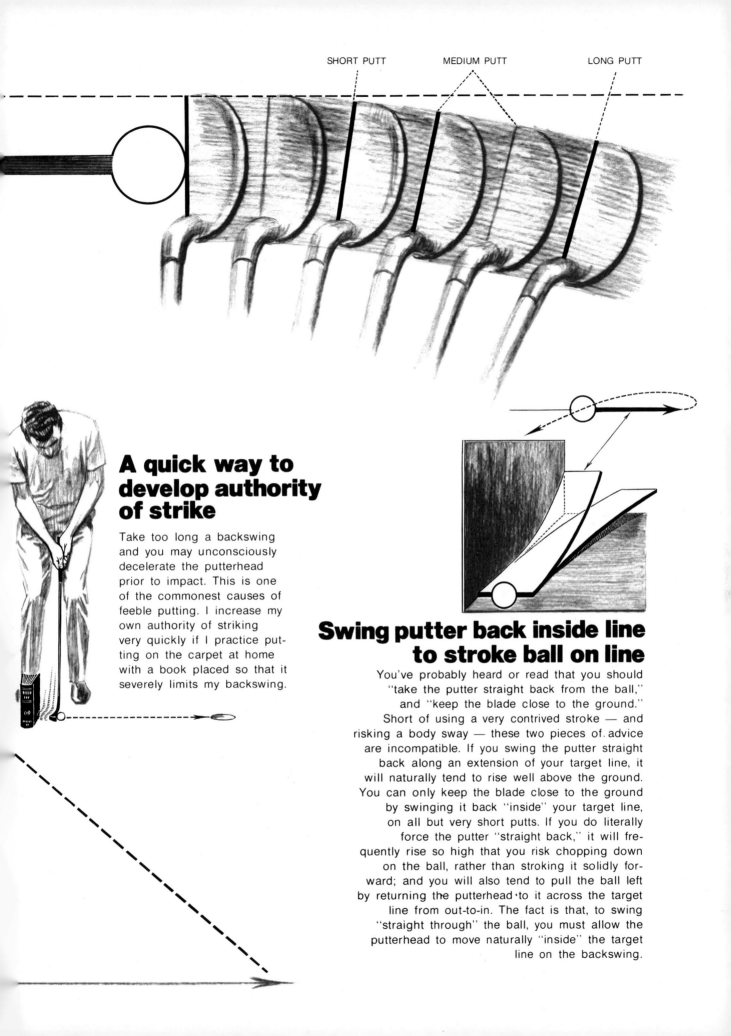

SHORT PUTT   MEDIUM PUTT   LONG PUTT

A quick way to develop authority of strike

Take too long a backswing and you may unconsciously decelerate the putterhead prior to impact. This is one of the commonest causes of feeble putting. I increase my own authority of striking very quickly if I practice putting on the carpet at home with a book placed so that it severely limits my backswing.

Swing putter back inside line to stroke ball on line

You've probably heard or read that you should "take the putter straight back from the ball," and "keep the blade close to the ground." Short of using a very contrived stroke — and risking a body sway — these two pieces of advice are incompatible. If you swing the putter straight back along an extension of your target line, it will naturally tend to rise well above the ground. You can only keep the blade close to the ground by swinging it back "inside" your target line, on all but very short putts. If you do literally force the putter "straight back," it will frequently rise so high that you risk chopping down on the ball, rather than stroking it solidly forward; and you will also tend to pull the ball left by returning the putterhead·to it across the target line from out-to-in. The fact is that, to swing "straight through" the ball, you must allow the putterhead to move naturally "inside" the target line on the backswing.

stroke, the arms swing farther and more freely on the backswing, and the hands at some stage pass the left wrist on the follow-through. But the principles remain the same.

All the accent on "square" these days has put the idea in many golfers' minds that a prime putting goal is to swing the putter straight back from the ball and straight through, and one often sees people trying to do just that, even on 50-yarders. I am sure it is a bad thought for the majority of people. Only on the very shortest putt, using the shortest stroke, is it possible to swing the putterhead straight back and straight through along the target-line without being so deliberate and method-conscious as to inhibit the whole stroking movement, and thereby forget the most essential item — *striking* the ball.

What actually happens on a putt of any length is that the clubhead moves straight back for a very short distance, then **inside** the line — just as it does on any other kind of golf swing. In fact, only from this kind of backswing is it possible to hit **straight through** the ball at impact with a square putter face. During my days as a tournament player I was a poor putter because I strived to follow the advice drummed into me as a youngster — to "keep the clubhead moving back and through on a straight line and the blade close to the ground." On a putt of anything more than 10 feet, it is **impossible** to do both these things without considerable body movement, which makes it difficult to swing the putter head smoothly and solidly into the ball.

On medium and long putts the clubhead must be swung back so far that, if it is moved strictly along the target line, it has to rise well off the ground. Alternatively, if the clubhead is to be held close to the ground, the club has to swing inside the target line on a gentle arc to that line (as it does on every other golf shot). The latter, in fact, is exactly what should happen. The club should start straight back, swing slightly inside, then return along the same inside-to-straight-through path.

To prove this, put a ball down on the carpet a few inches away from a wall and line up to putt as if the hole was the same distance from the wall but 10 or 12 feet away. In making your stroke the putter head should never be closer to the wall than it is at address; you will find that, the farther the club is swung back — if you swing it naturally — the greater the distance between wall and clubhead becomes. Find out for yourself how much your putterhead must come inside on the backswing in order to return to the ball traveling along the target line.

One of the commonest putting faults is decelerating the clubhead before impact. It usually happens because the backswing is too long and/or too fast, then everything has to slow down on the through-swing to prevent the ball being hit too far. It is impossible to make crisp contact with a decelerating putterhead. To learn to accelerate it, practice making the ball cover a specific distance with a stroke a little shorter than you'd normally need. Abbreviating the backswing teaches authoritative striking faster than anything I know of. I used to do it for hours at home on the carpet. I'd take a book and place it only an inch or two behind the putter, then try to hit the ball crisply to my mark without having touched the book on the backswing. If you do this for a quarter of an hour a day, concentrating especially on keeping the left wrist firm, you will soon discover what the professionals mean when they talk of "rap" putting.

Two judgment factors are involved in putting — line and distance. Far more putts are missed because of incorrect distance than incorrect direction. Most people are able to read a green reasonably well — certainly well enough to get down in two putts most of the time. Their real problem is hitting the ball way short or way past the hole. Why is it so difficult to judge distance? The main reason is that few people strike every putt the same way, more or less on the same spot on the putterface; and, until a consistent strike with the head of the putter is mastered, the ball will not travel an equal distance for a particular length of backswing or force of hit. That's why it is essential to develop a repeating stroke that swings the putterhead into the ball from the inside. This is a matter of practice and "feel." But remember, too, that "line" is often governed by pace. There can be four different "lines" to a five-foot putt, depending on how hard you hit it. So spend a majority of your practice time hitting the ball a certain distance. Mark a line or lay a club down and hit the ball to stop exactly at that mark.

I am often asked if it is possible for a really poor putter ever to become a good one. I think it is. I have never naturally been a good putter, but, in the period 1952-56, I made myself one by sheer study and willpower and practice. I am sure this is true, too, of many of the world's top players. They have followed a simple system: first, develop a sound method, then practice it endlessly.

So many of us simply do not **strike** our putts — indeed, by comparison with the Americans, feebleness on the greens seems

95

to be a national British weakness. I am certain that ball size has a great deal to do with this, and that we shall never become as able and confident on the short shots as the Americans until we use the 1.68-inch ball. But another factor undoubtedly has been the British predilection for many generations with *stroking* the golf ball. Our whole concept of golf technique has been based on style, grace and ease. We have always tended to be as much concerned with how the thing looked as with how it worked.

Other nations do not have our long golfing heritage. They have sought efficiency of method, with small regard for appearances. The result is that they have evolved methods that may be less aesthetically attractive than ours, but often are more effective. This is true of putting just as it is of the long game. I remember, with amusement, the horror with which the "jab" putting technique of American pros, as some British experts called it, was greeted soon after the Second World War. It seemed to contradict every tenet ever advanced in Britain for getting the ball into the hole. But when we played the Americans, we learned quickly and painfully just how well the ugly-looking "jab" worked.

I'd never be dogmatic about the mechanics of the putting stroke. If you have a grip and a stance that work for you, guard them with your life, however odd and unorthodox they might seem to your friends. If you haven't, bear in mind the following:

The head is important. It must be kept **really** still if the ball is to be struck firmly and accurately. Set your head in one spot and hold it there as long as you can. Try to "hit and hark." Strike the ball and wait to hear it drop in the hole before you look up.

The arrangement of the hands on the club is a matter of personal preference, but I believe that when the palms are exactly opposed it is easier to strike squarely without rolling the clubface. The back of the left hand and the palm of the right hand should, ideally, "look at" the hole. Most good putters seem to use a palm grip with the left hand, the club running through the center of the hand. The right hand generally hangs on mostly in the fingers for maximum "feel." If you are a poor or indifferent putter, try holding the club tight rather than soft. That excellent American putter, Jack Burke, worked with a tight grip and a "rap" stroke. "I'm always going to twitch some," he said, "so I practice twitching!"

Stance for putting, like the grip, is a personal matter, but I would suggest a square alignment: feet and shoulders parallel to the line of the shot; feet about nine inches apart; weight solidly on the heels and soles of both feet; the ball placed opposite a point between the left toe and the center of the feet. This sort of set-up will generally bring the elbows in to rest on the thighs — tucked in and supported.

However you stand, make sure your eyes are either over or behind the ball — never ahead of it so that you are looking down on the hole side of the ball. You must be able to "sense" the direction you want the ball to take as you line up, and that is easiest to do when you look from behind the shot. Jack Nicklaus best personifies this kind of set-up. His eyes are behind the ball; he sees the back of it and hits it away from him.

What sort of putter should you use? The choice is highly individual. A mallet is often thought to be best for slow, wet greens, a blade for smooth, fast greens. Probably the best answer is to use the putter that gives you the best feel, or the one in which you have most confidence. But don't stick with it if your putting goes off. I'm a great believer in changing putters if I'm putting badly. However, if you follow this advice and have more than one putter, make them as different as possible from each other. A blade and a mallet are good alternatives.

One final thought. Always try to spend at least five minutes putting before an important round — and practice the middle and long-distance putts, not the short ones. This is the best way to induce rhythm and "feel." If you practice short putts without being under pressure to hole them, you are apt to miss a few simply because they aren't important, which does nothing for your confidence.

TROUBLE

Ways out of rough stuff

Every golfer lands in trouble. How well he gets out depends on his mental equilibrium, his common sense, and often, in the long run, his sheer physical strength.

The first rule of playing from trouble is simply to get out. This is where mental equilibrium is so big a factor. Many golfers become so angry or dismayed when a bad miss lands them in cabbage that all reason departs. They call upon temper or belief in miracles to make amends. Neither are reliable factors in golf.

The first thing to do if you are in trouble is to keep calm. The second is to decide what is definitely possible in the way of recovery, what is just probable, and what is impossible. If the situation is impossible, take an unplayable lie penalty and drop away or go back and play another ball. If it is just probable, and the state of the match or the game suggests a gamble, have a go. Most of the time stick to what is definitely possible — even if it means, as it often does, the shortest route back to the fairway.

The deeper the trouble — grass, bushes, gorse, heather, bramble, bracken, etc. — the more difficult it is to get out. In all these instances, whatever the ball lies in will wrap around the club's hosel before the ball is contacted, slowing the club down, stopping it completely, or twisting the face off-line to the left.

Sheer physical strength is probably the only reliable method of shifting a ball from a really bad spot. If you lack it, play safe.

Most of the time, however, trouble means rough grass of varying depth and texture bordering fairways. The problem here is how cleanly the clubface can be applied to the back of the ball, and how the ball will behave when grass comes between it and the clubface at impact.

Backspin is what controls a golf ball — makes it fly in a certain trajectory and stop in a certain manner — and backspin is best applied by the clubface hitting the ball a clean, slightly descending blow. Anything coming between the ball and the clubface at impact reduces backspin, thereby reducing your control over the shot.

The normal effect of grass coming between clubface and ball, because of the reduced backspin, is to make the ball fly lower and run farther when it lands.

A ball lying reasonably well in dry, light grass or semi-rough may be played normally, taking into account only the foregoing, i.e., that less club might be needed than when the same length or type of shot is played

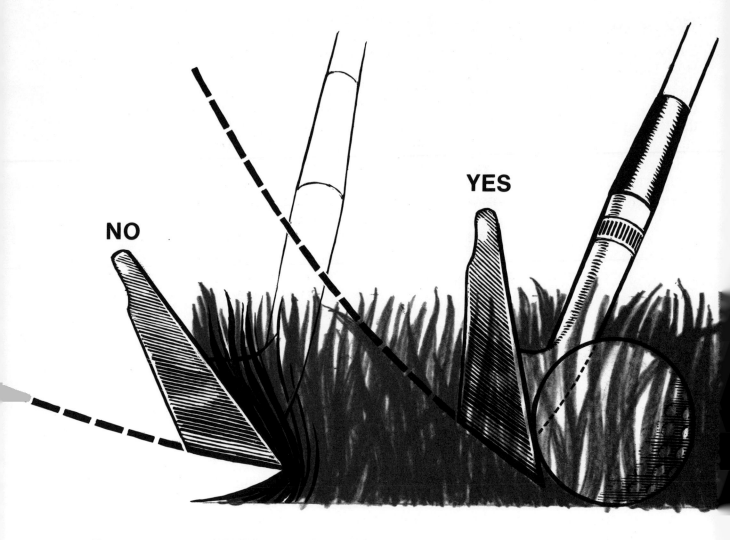

Strike DOWN–don't sweep

In any kind of rough, the more garbage you contact before the ball the less effective the shot. So don't sweep the clubhead back and through. Swing it sharply up and down and through the ball as cleanly as possible.

from the fairway.

If the ball is nestling down in long or lush grass, leaving no clear path for the clubhead to meet the back of it, the only way to remove it effectively is by a steep, descending blow with a lofted club. This shot should be played with the clubface opened a few degrees at address. Swing the club up with an early wrist-cock to produce a steep arc. In the downswing see that your hands lead the clubhead, and that your grip remains firm. The ball needs almost to be "punched" out — struck a firm descending blow. Don't worry about follow-through. Look at the back of the ball and try to get the clubface down onto it as cleanly as possible.

Although it doesn't always appear so, one of the most difficult trouble shots is that presented when a ball tees itself up in light rough — anything from half an inch to two inches above the ground. The great danger here lies in swinging the clubface underneath the ball, ballooning it weakly high in the air. Here the only real safeguard is to watch the ball carefully and use a deep-faced club (the driver is ideal if distance is required).

Another poser is the ball under an obstacle such as the branches of a tree. Take a long-iron, de-loft it even more by playing the ball opposite your right toe, hood the clubface,

and punch down into the ball, making sure that your hands lead at impact. Allow for a great deal of run.

An experienced and thoughtful golfer is always ready to make up shots to extricate himself from trouble. So long as you do not scoop or scrape at the ball, almost any sort of blow is permissible, and all kinds can be contrived to escape trouble.

A putter can be used in all sorts of situations where a longer or more lofted club won't work — including bunker play when the trap lacks a sharp lip and the lie is good.

A ball lying very close to a wall or a tree can be bounced off the obstacle to get it clear — but be careful it does not strike you or the club on the rebound. A ball in a bush can often be bunted out backwards between the legs by chopping down on it vertically. Reversed so that the toe points down, a right-handed club can be used to knock out a ball from a spot where only a left-handed swing will do.

You can get a lot of distance out of grass if height is not necessary by using an inelegant shot with a medium iron. Set up with the ball well back towards your right foot and weight predominantly on your left side. Hood the clubface slightly and, again, pick up the club quickly in the backswing to keep it out of the grass, then literally **smash**

101

it down into the back of the ball with your hands and arms. This action will not produce a good-looking golf shot, but it **will** get the ball moving on a low trajectory that will send it running a long way. Allow for the ball to hook.

When faced with a shot which must go either over or around an obstruction, the lie of the ball and your own ability as a golfer are the factors that should decide your course of action. It is probably easier for most golfers to hit a high shot than a deliberate hook or slice, but you must have a good lie to be sure of bringing off a really high shot. Play the ball well forward, set your hands level with the clubface at address, and use plenty of hand and arm action in the backswing and downswing.

If the lie is not good, then the easiest shot for the majority of golfers is probably a deliberate slice. Take one more club that you would normally need for the same distance. Set-up with the clubface open (right of target), and align your feet and shoulders left of target. Swing the club steeply up and down with the hands and arms on the out-to-in swing path that your open address position establishes, and **ensure that your hips keep going right through the downswing to prevent the hands from closing the clubface at impact.**

If you are a natural hooker and thus confident about bending the ball from right-to-left, take one **less** club than normal and aim yourself and the club right of target. The ball should be well back in the stance with both the feet and shoulders closed and the hands leading the clubface. Make a full shoulder turn in the backswing and swing the clubhead into the ball with your arms and hands in good time.

One of the most difficult shots in golf is a short pitch from thick, lush grass — especially when there is little margin for error as often happens when a bunker intervenes between you and the pin, and the ball must fly the necessary distance but still land softly. The grooming of many American courses makes this a common problem for the U.S. tournament professionals, and some of them have developed a rather special type of stroke to overcome it.

The essential club for this shot is a broad-soled sand wedge; the essential attribute in the player is confidence, which comes from practice; and the critical part of the technique is to hit a little way behind the ball with an open clubface, as in a standard "splash" shot from sand.

If you have rough close up to your greens, it would be worth experimenting with this stroke. Play the ball well forward, open the clubface slightly at address, make a slow and easy swing with plenty of arm action, the club going back a little outside the target line. Then swing the clubhead down a little way behind the ball — being sure to keep it going right through grass and ball.

How to play the three basic bunker shots

It is sometimes said that splashing the ball from sand is the easiest shot in the game. I don't go all the way with that idea, but I would agree that, given a basic understanding of the problems and methods of getting the ball out of sand, the average player can at least overcome the fear that seems to paralyze him every time his ball lands in a bunker. And that alone will give him a 50 per cent better chance of getting out of the sand with only one blow struck.

Through the green you play golf with one basic swing. On the "type" shots made necessary by getting into trouble, this repetition breaks down somewhat. Careful study of the situation, an accurate assessment of what sort of club and stroke are necessary, understanding of how varying conditions will affect the behavior of the club and the ball, and confidence in the method finally chosen to execute the shot — these are the essentials if you are to master the hazards as well as the mowed sections of the golf course.

Regarding sand, the first thing to emphasize is that there is more than one type of bunker shot. There are, in fact, basically three, and they can be classified as the shots played:

1. When the ball is bunkered close to the green and the lie is good.

2. When the lie is bad, i.e., the ball is plugged, badly cupped or otherwise nastily situated.

3. When distance is required.

The "Splash" Shot

The first of these situations requires the basic bunker shot, which some people call an "explosion" or "blast" shot but which I prefer to call a "splash" shot. It is the shot that so impresses golf crowds when they see professionals knock the ball stiff to the pin from sand. It is a relatively easy shot to play, **once you've established confidence.**

If there is a secret to playing the "splash" shot, it lies in knowing how far behind the ball to apply the clubhead, and then having the confidence to do it. In this shot the ball itself is **never** contacted by the clubface. The sand is struck behind the ball and the sand-wedge, due to its heavy protruding flange, splashes or skids through the sand beneath the ball, which

103

Control distance by your set-up

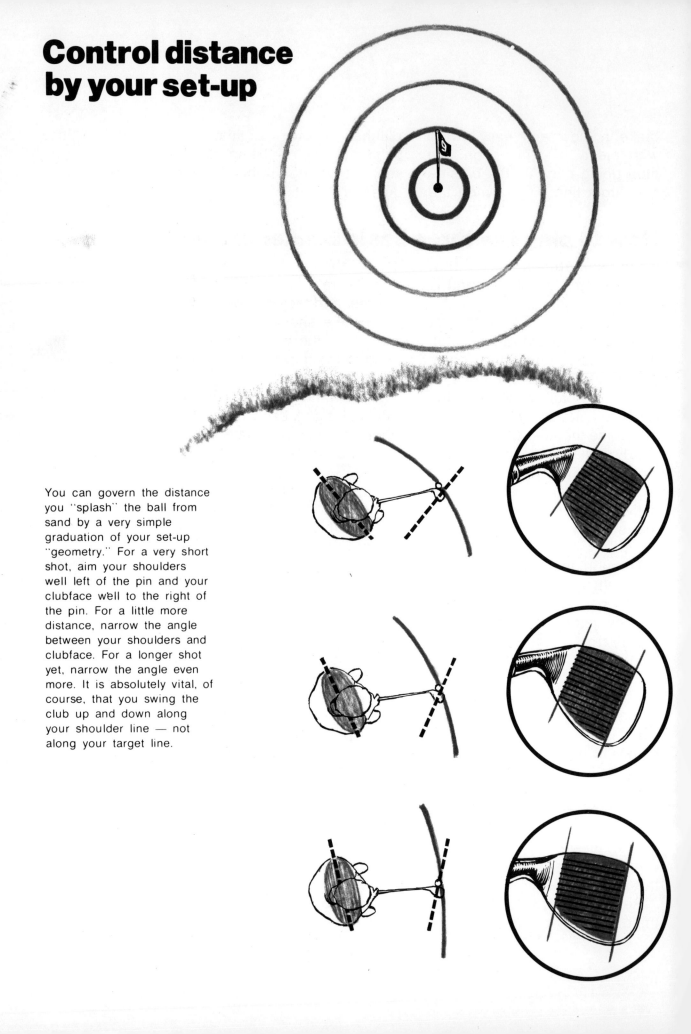

You can govern the distance you "splash" the ball from sand by a very simple graduation of your set-up "geometry." For a very short shot, aim your shoulders well left of the pin and your clubface well to the right of the pin. For a little more distance, narrow the angle between your shoulders and clubface. For a longer shot yet, narrow the angle even more. It is absolutely vital, of course, that you swing the club up and down along your shoulder line — not along your target line.

flies up out of the bunker literally on a cushion of sand.

How far behind the ball should you hit the sand? I can't tell you. The exact distance depends on the flight required and the condition of the sand, and you can only learn to judge these two factors through practice and experience. But the distance will vary between two and four inches, less sand generally being taken the farther the ball must travel.

As in every golf shot, the correct set-up is vital. Position the ball opposite the left heel, and make sure that both your feet and shoulders are set up open — your left side pulled back from the target line. Open the face of the club, fractionally for a normal trajectory, wide for a higher shot. Then swing the club smoothly along your open shoulder line, i.e., out-to-in. I repeat, *smoothly along your shoulder line*. Make a full, free swing with the hands and arms. There need be no deliberate turn of the shoulders, but your knees should be flexed and your upper body relaxed.

In order to hit under and through the ball, you must be sure to get your hips moving and turning to the left as the clubhead swings down and through. Only by moving the hips can the face of the club be kept open so that it slides through the sand under the ball. If your hips are static, the down-

swing becomes a movement of the hands and arms only. Then, as the clubhead approaches the ball, the arms start to move around the body and the clubface closes and digs into the sand. Don't swing **at** the ball — think of skimming the clubface through the sand **under** the ball and floating it out. The shot is a gentle splash, not a thunderous blast.

I mentioned that the distance the ball travels is controlled by how far behind it the club cuts into the sand. For me, a simpler way of varying distance lies in altering the degree to which I open both the clubface and my body alignment. For a longish shot, I open my set-up and clubface minimally. For a very short shot, I set-up with my shoulders and feet aimed way left of target and my clubface aimed way right. It is essential if you seek to control distance by this method to ensure that you always *swing along the open shoulder line you've* established.

If the sand is very hard, position the ball more centrally between your feet and cut **down** and across it a little more.

From a Bad Lie

Many golfers, good golfers among them, make the mistake, when the ball is plugged in sand, of opening the clubface even more than they would for a normal bunker shot. That is

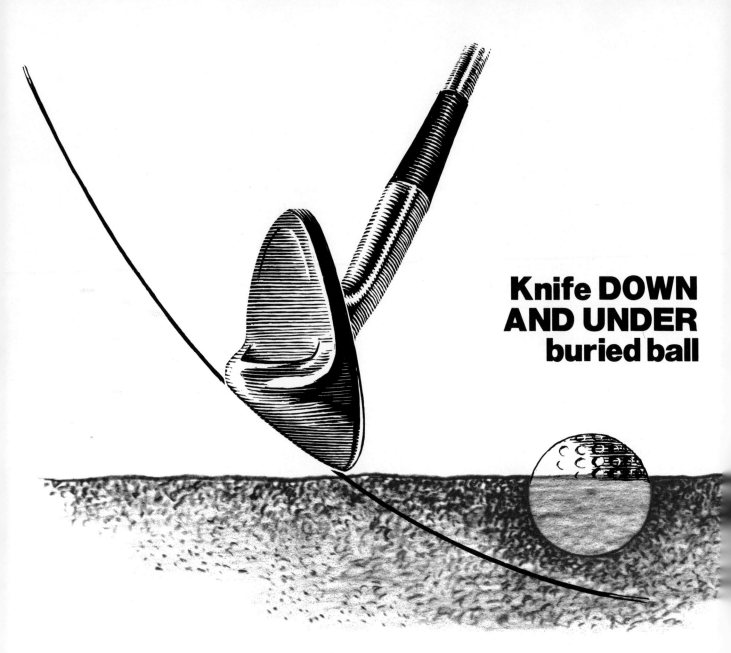

Knife DOWN AND UNDER buried ball

Any time your ball is partly or completely buried in sand, the only sure way to get it out is to swing the clubhead well down and under the ball. The easiest way to do that is to close the clubface so that its sharp leading edge will "knife" through the sand when you swing sharply down behind the ball.

exactly the reverse of what is needed. The heavy flange of the wedge makes a relatively shallow skid through the sand, and fails to get under the ball, which generally stays in sand.

This shot is very much a strong "pick and chop" action. It is not a good-looking golf shot, as is the splash shot, and it is rarely possible to make a fancy follow-through.

The hands should always be **ahead** of the clubface at address on this shot, and they must still be leading at impact. The swing must be steep, and very often, on a bad plug in wet or heavy sand, a lot of physical effort may be necessary really to thump the club down and through the sand under the ball.

One problem of this shot is that the ball, lacking backspin, will roll a good deal, making distance judgment difficult. Practice is necessary to know what can be done with such a shot, but if you haven't much room be prepared to go well past the hole.

Going for Distance

The most important factor in going for distance from sand is correct club selection. So often I see players with the ball lying well back in a shallow bunker take a straight-faced club, then, in mid-swing, suddenly think they are going to catch the trap's front lip. The inevitable result is that they try to flick the ball off the sand. That causes the wrists to release too early, widens the downswing, and brings the clubhead into the sand behind the ball. Disaster — always!

It is vital if you want distance from a bunker to hit ball first, sand second — just as one does with an iron from the fairway. To do that, it is imperative that you have no fear in your mind that you haven't enough loft on the club to lift the ball over the bunker's lip. This is your limiting factor in the distance you can get from sand. You have to take the club which will, **without doubt,** clear the lip, even when you de-loft it a little by positioning the ball farther back than normal towards your rear foot, with the hands three to four inches ahead of the clubface at address.

This set-up, with the weight predominantly on your forward foot, ensures that the ball will be hit first, sand second. From this position swing normally and forcefully, endeavoring above all to lead the clubface into the ball with your hands.

Never be over-ambitious on this shot. Err on the safe side.

My overall advice on bunker play is that you give a little time to practice it. Sand really isn't the terror it seems to most club golfers. If you will spend an hour hitting shots from sand, I'll guarantee your fear of it will disappear.

Choose club
with loft
to spare

To get distance from a
bunker, you must hit the ball
before the sand. To ensure
that you do so necessitates
playing the ball farther back
in your stance than normal,
which has the effect of decreasing the loft of whatever
club you choose. So make sure
you choose a club which —
even when de-lofted — will
carry the ball clear of the
lip of the bunker.

Coping with slopes

UPHILL LIE

BALL ABOVE FEET

DOWNHILL LIE

BALL BELOW FEET

Coping with slopes

Uphill lie (hitting up the slope)

Stand perpendicular to the slope, which will drop your rear shoulder lower than usual. You are now in a position where you can swing parallel to the slope, without hitting into it after you have made contact with the ball. Swing **down** the slope in the backswing and **up** the slope in the through-swing. This will leave most of your weight on your rear side, and from this position it is very easy to hook the ball; so aim a little right of target. Hitting uphill also increases the height of the shot, which reduces its length, so take more club than normal.

Downhill lie (hitting down the slope)

Again, set yourself perpendicular to the slope, which will put most of your weight on your left side, and your hands ahead of the ball. This shot requires a quick pick-up of the club in the backswing and a hit down the slope. Any attempt to scoop the ball into the air will be fatal. You must drive **down and through** and really "chase" the clubhead after the ball down the slope. This shot is easiest to play with the well-lofted clubs. If you do make solid contact, the ball will travel lower and thus tend to run farther than from a level lie. So make the appropriate allowance in your club selection.

Ball above feet

With the ball higher than your feet, you will have to stand more erect than usual at address and farther away from the ball. This will necessitate swinging more around your body in a flatter plane than from a level lie. Such an action tends to produce a hook, so aim right of target to allow for it.

Ball below feet

You must bend over farther to reach the ball, and therefore stand closer to it. This will set you in a position where your swing plane must become more upright than usual. It also restricts your body turn, so the swing becomes predominantly a hands and arms movement. The resulting steepness can lead to a slice, and you should aim left of target to allow for it.

THE
MAJOR
FAULTS

You can stop slicing forever in five minutes!

I'm writing this chapter hot — and hot under the collar — from some marathon teaching sessions at my Golf Centers. Never before have I realized quite so emphatically how major a problem the slice in golf is. It really is the golfer's curse! I'm sure that at least 80 per cent of the people I've seen in these sessions have sliced ever since they started trying to play the game. But the really devastating thing is their ignorance of why they slice. Not one in 50 really knows what causes his ball time and again to start left and dribble away weakly to the right.

"Why do you slice?" I ask, and usually I get the same answer: "Because I hit across the ball." This is a **contributory** factor in a slice, but it is not the basic cause. Hitting across the ball may produce a pull, or, if the clubface is shut, a quick hook. The **basic** cause of a slice — the common factor in every shot started left that bends right towards the end of its flight — is **a clubface that is open to the swing line at impact.**

You slice because the clubface is open — pointing right of the direction in which your club is traveling — as you hit the ball. Please, *please* get that fact implanted in your golfing consciousness if you really want to eradicate this disastrous shot.

The slice, like so many other faults, stems basically from the grip. Golf is such a difficult and frustrating game for so many people because they can never be bothered to develop an effective grip. Indeed, the very last thing the average golfer wants to be told by a pro is to change his grip. It's too much bother, it's too uncomfortable, it couldn't possibly make that much difference, and anyway, he's sure his faults are in his backswing, or his downswing, or his follow-through. Because he has never thought out the simple ballistics of the game, he doesn't appreciate the fundamental and very simple fact that **everything** in golf stems from the way the clubface meets the ball.

The habitual slicers are the worst in this way. They go on playing with a hold on the club that brings the clubface to the ball in an open position. Then, because with this grip if they stand square to the target line their shots go straight out to the right, subconsciously they angle themselves around until they are facing miles left of the target. The effect of this shoulder alignment is actually to increase the slice potential of their grip. Then, of course, they swing out-to-in across the ball — the only way they can swing with such a set-up. With the clubface now very open to this line of swing, nothing but a sliced shot can **possibly** result.

I will repeat once again what I must have said ten thousand times: you **must** find a grip that returns the clubface square to your line of swing at impact. If you will not or cannot do this, your golf will always be inconsistent and, in most cases, downright lousy.

In teaching I am often able to stop a lot of golfers slicing inside five minutes. I do it simply by persuading — sometimes forcing! — them to aim the clubface at the target, with the right shoulder pulled well around — probably six or eight inches back from the position it has been in. This in itself immediately improves their grip, because it pulls the hands at address away from the left side and brings them more towards the center of the body. From this address position, I then ask the pupil to have the feeling in the takeaway that he is closing the clubface. This is essential in the early cure of a slicer, because, in his previous action, with his very open body set-up and hands well forward, he is almost certain to have been rolling the clubface open with his hands and wrists in the takeaway — the only way he can get the club away from the ball on what seems to be the right path when his body is aligned miles to the left of his intended target.

The first essential, then, for the consistent slicer is to square his shoulders to the target line at address. Often this will give him the feeling that he is closed — aiming right of target. But it is **imperative** that he gets his shoulders square, and he will usually only do this if, at first, he feels closed in his upper-body alignment.

The golfer now has made room for his arms to swing up — and consequently down — on the inside. He no longer feels the need to make the pronounced rotary movement of his body to get the club back on the inside that was necessary from his open-shouldered address position — a movement that produced a reciprocal rotary body swivel on the downswing that threw the club outside the target line. It is easy for him now to develop the feeling of swinging his arms **up on the inside** in the backswing. From here they will surely swing **down on the inside**, causing his right shoulder to trail his arms instead of leading them.

I guarantee that anyone who can master this set-up and armswing will stop slicing in five minutes. I also guarantee that he or she will be staggered and delighted by the feeling of solid striking that results. Indeed, many golfers realize after a few dozen shots like this that, for the first time in their lives, they

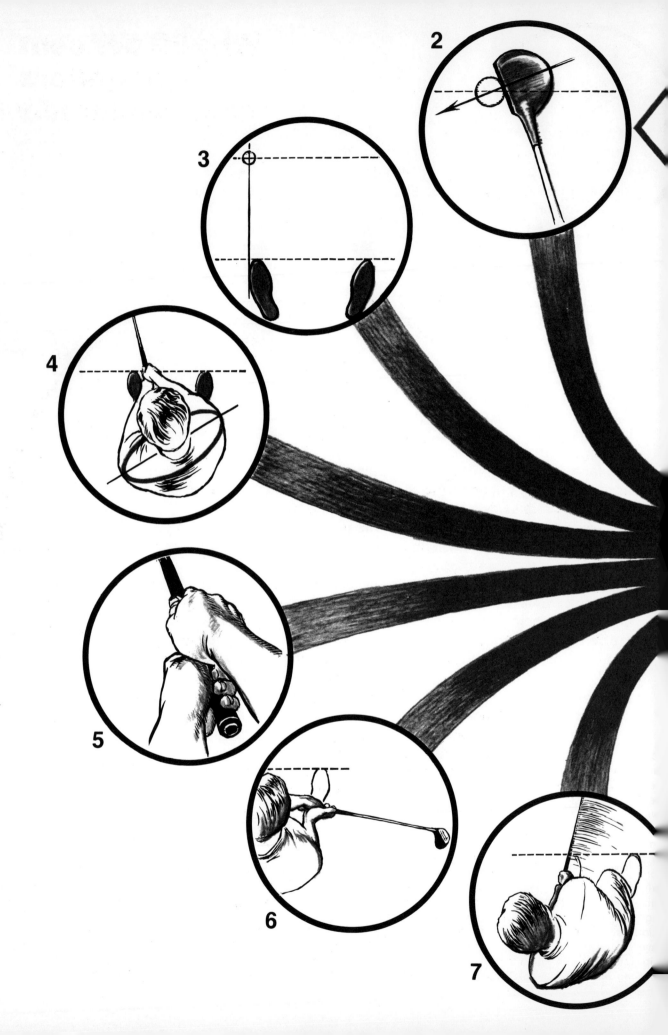

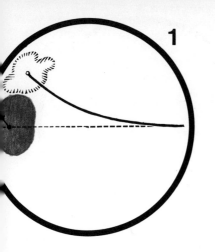

Why 80 per cent of golfers slice repeatedly

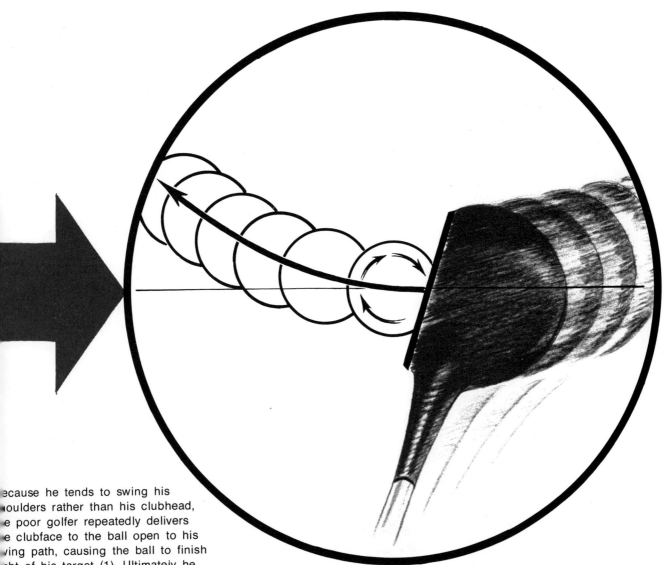

ecause he tends to swing his
houlders rather than his clubhead,
e poor golfer repeatedly delivers
e clubface to the ball open to his
ving path, causing the ball to finish
ght of his target (1). Ultimately he
ms the clubface left at address, in
instinctive effort to stop the ball
om going right (2). This sets the
ll too far forward in his stance (3).
is, in turn, forces his shoulders to
gn left of target (4). His ball po-
ion and his open shoulders jointly
ve the effect of "weakening" his
ip, relative to his target line (5).
owing he should swing the club

"straight back" from the ball, but
blocked from doing so by his open
shoulder alignment, he instinctively
maneuvers the club "inside" on
the backswing, by either spinning his
upper body or pulling his arms sharply
"inside," usually fanning open the
clubface with his hands in both cases (6).
At the top of the backswing his body
"rebounds," throwing his right shoulder,

and his hands, arms and the club outwards toward the target line (7). Swung
thus, the club can *only* approach the ball
steeply and across the target line from
outside to inside. Usually the face of
the club will be open to its path, causing
a slice. If the face is square to the
swing path, the ball pulls left. If the
clubface is closed to the swing
path, the ball pull-hooks.

are playing golf in a way that enables them to apply the clubhead fast and solidly into **the back** of the ball. It is a whole new experience for most.

The next stage, of course, is to modify the action according to the flight of the ball, by experimenting with the grip and shoulder alignment. If the ball hooks, the shoulders may be a little too closed at address. If it is pushed straight out to the right, the grip may be a little weak, and the hands can be moved slightly more to the right. Trial and error is necessary to consistently produce straight shots — but it must, for the congenital slicer, be within the framework of a square or slightly closed shoulder position at address and no independent action of the hands and wrists in the takeaway of the club, instead of a swivel of the body and roll of the wrists.

Another vital factor for the inveterate slicer is head position at address. Most slicers set their heads too far to the left — over or even in front of the ball — which forces them into the open-shouldered, open-bladed set-up that guarantees a slice. They should observe how the very good golfer *always* sets his head behind the ball, and looks into the back of it — the bit he wants to hit.

If you stand so that you must look at the front (or even the top) of the ball, not only are you set-up for an across-the-ball swing, but your whole left side is almost certainly going to collapse as you start down. Looking at the back of the ball from behind it establishes a strong left side. Remember, when your game goes bad, that the set of the head affects the shoulder alignment and that the alignment of the shoulders has a big effect on the type of shots you will hit.

We cannot get away from the fact that golf is basically a matter of grip and set-up. If you set yourself so that you must swing across the ball with an open clubface, you are doomed to slice — no other shot is possible. And the problem is that golfers who don't understand how important the set-up is aggravate their faults by purely instinctive movements.

The slicer, indeed, is the supreme example. The ball goes to the right, and the more it does the more he sets himself to the left — shoulders open, head in front of the ball, and, worst of all, a slicer's weak grip. Eventually, poor soul, he gets to the stage where the only thing he can possibly do is produce feeble banana shots from far left to far right.

Thus, the slicer's first task must **always** be to get himself into a square address position — shoulders, hips, knees and feet parallel to the target line, or even slightly "inside" it. This will enable him to grip the club in a way that will let him swing the clubface through the ball looking at the target.

Help for hookers
–and pullers who think they're hookers

The fact that there are fewer "natural" hookers in golf than slicers is very little consolation to the player whose every other shot darts sharply off to the left. True, he is likely to be a better golfer than his opposite number, but at times he will be in such a mess as to be virtually a non-starter. A genuine hook — a hard-hit ball swinging violently left — is a shot ranking in disaster quotient with the shank.

The slicer, although a weak striker and short hitter, can usually at least remain in the park, because a "cut" ball flies, lands and rolls more softly than a hooked ball. It is for this reason that so many professionals and first-class amateurs favor a slight fade, and why at the highest levels of the game one hears so much about "blocking" shots. To the good player, especially if he hits the ball a long way, a hook is a constant threat.

Even though a hooker usually has some knowledge of golf, like the slicer his problem stems from lack of basic analysis of cause and effect. He may have thought hard and long about his swing, but he hasn't taken the problem to its root, which is the direction in which the clubhead approaches the ball and the alignment of its face at impact.

I have proof of this daily. Good players come to me and say they are hooking. I ask them to do so. They hit a few shots, and, true enough, the ball goes to the left. But in many cases it does not "bend" to the left. It flies straight to the left, or starts left and then goes more left. These shots are not hooks. They are pulls and pulled hooks. And the important thing is that they do not stem from the sort of action that produces a genuine hook. They stem, indeed, from the very opposite, from a slicer's action, an out-to-in swing. All they lack is the slicer's open clubface at impact. If these self-described "hookers" were to hit the ball with an open clubface, they would in fact slice. If they were just to swing the club through the ball in the right direction, all would be well.

In golf, it really does help to know what you are actually doing before you try to alter it!

The genuinely hooked shot starts to the *right* of the target, then swings away to the left. If its turn is gentle, the shot is described as being "drawn" —

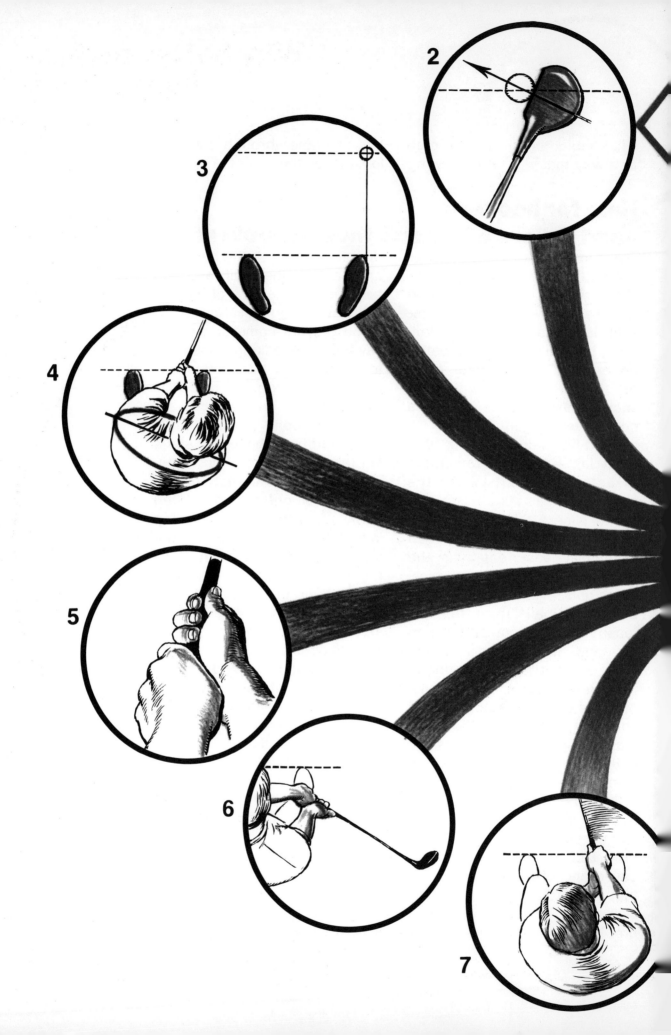

Why better golfers fight a hook

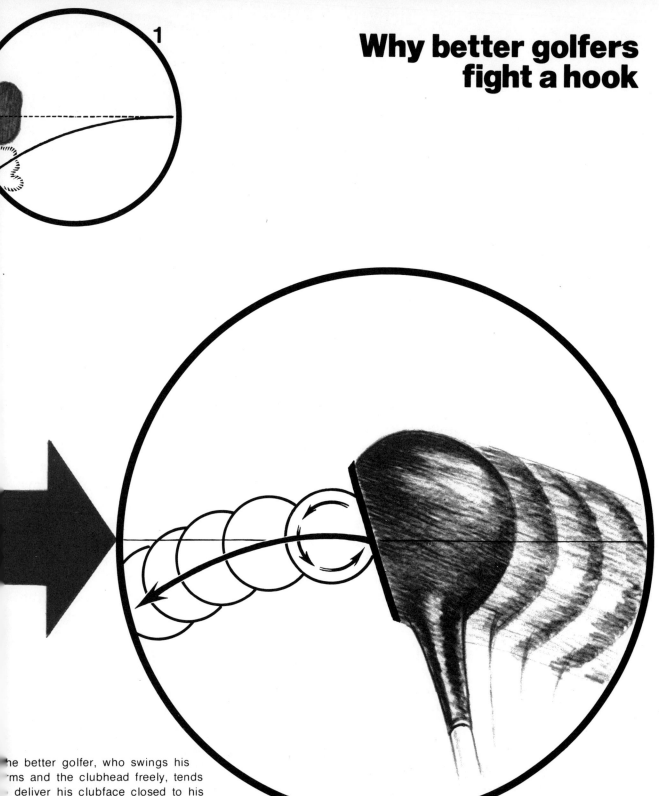

he better golfer, who swings his rms and the clubhead freely, tends deliver his clubface closed to his ving path during impact, causing e ball to finish left of target (1). e then aims the clubface right of rget at address, in an instinctive fort to stop the ball from going t (2). This sets the ball too far ck in his stance (3). This, in turn, igns his shoulders right of target (4). s rearward ball position and his osed shoulders jointly have the ef- ct of "strengthening" his grip, rela- e to his target line (5). His strong

grip and closed shoulders cause him to swing his body and the club too much "inside" on the backswing (6). Coming down, he cannot make room for his arms to swing past his body by leading the through-swing with the legs and hips, thus his wrists must roll over rapidly — to square the clubface. (7). The club can *only* arrive

at the ball traveling on a very shallow arc, from inside to outside the target line. The clubface is usually closed to his swing path by the golfer's rolling wrists, thus the ball hooks. If the club- face is square to the swing path, the ball is pushed straight right. If the face is open to the swing path, the ball is push-sliced.

perhaps the most useful "shape" for the average player, in that the kind of spin imparted to the ball increases both carry and run. If the turn is violent, the shot is disastrous at any level of the game. In both instances, and in every variation in between, the shot is made by the club coming to the ball from inside the target line with the face at impact closed to the line of swing.

(I might add here, for the benefit of people who hit the ball straight to the right and think they slice, that in fact they have a hooker's action, except that the clubface is square to their inside-out swing.)

It should be clear by now that the hooker hooks because something in his action brings his club to the ball on an "inside" path with the face closed to that path. What is that something, and how does he adjust it?

We must go back, as always, to the clubface. If it comes into the ball closed, an in-to-out swing will naturally follow, due to the golfer instinctively trying to swing the club to the right to counteract the "bend" in his shots. The hooker's first job, then, is simple: to square his clubface, which will make the ball fly straight along its starting path — in the same direction as he is swinging. This usually requires nothing more than some intelligent grip adjustment.

If you are a true hooker it is more than likely that you close the clubface at impact because your grip is too "strong" — your left hand is too much on top and your right too much underneath the shaft. Move both hands bit by bit to the left. It will feel uncomfortable for a while, but it will be worth the effort in the long run. A loose grip with the left hand very often closes the clubface, too, so make sure your hands work as a unit during the swing.

Persevering like this, you will eventually find that the ball, instead of starting right and turning left, starts right and continues that way. You have now swapped your hook for a push. Don't be disappointed. You have made the first of two adjustments, and are now ready to tackle the second.

If the ball now flies straight, your hands must be returning the clubface square to the line of your swing. It follows, therefore, that if the ball is not going where you think you are aiming, either your aim or your direction of swing is wrong. In this case you are pushing the ball straight to the right of your intended target. What does that mean? Simply that you are aiming to the right of the target when you set-up to the shot, in order to allow for your old hook, and thus are swinging the club along that line of aim — i.e., too much from inside to outside the proper ball-to-target line.

Your second task, therefore, is simple: aim and set yourself correctly. Arrange your feet, knees, hips and shoulders — especially shoulders — parallel to the target line with your club-face looking squarely at the tar-

get. As a hooker, you may feel as though you are now aiming miles left. You can check your feet by lining up with a club on the ground. Get someone to check your shoulders by laying a club across them after you've taken your stance.

If you top shots, your swing is too 'steep'

Ask golfers what causes a topped shot and most will immediately say "head up." You hear it time and again on golf courses all over the world. One member of a fourball scuttles a shot along the ground. "Head up!" exclaim the other three. They haven't actually seen their chum lift his head — indeed, they may not even have been watching him swing. But that doesn't matter. It has to be "head up."

Usually they are wrong. Lifting the head can cause the body to lift also, and when this happens it is true that the ball may be topped. But only a small proportion of thinly-hit shots stem from such a movement. Even if you anchored their heads in cement, a great many poor players would still manage to top the ball quite effectively — because the fault is not in their superstructure, it is built into their games by faulty swing patterns.

There are two basic causes of topping, they are closely allied to each other, and they emanate

from a particular kind of swing geometry.

To achieve flush contact with the back of the ball the club-head must be square and also travel through the impact zone on a reasonably shallow arc, moving from inside the target line, to straight along it, to inside again.

The chronic slicer never achieves either this shallow arc at impact or an inside-straight-through-inside clubhead path. For various reasons, usually a-rising from his set-up, he brings the club to the ball from well outside the target line — across the ball. Even the most elementary knowledge of geometrical principles indicates that this must severely steepen, or narrow, the arc described by the clubhead as it approaches the ball.

It can easily be understood that, even if the shot is reasonably effective — and 70 per cent of golfers play all their lives like this — the club has not hit the ball squarely in the back. To a greater or lesser degree, impact

123

has been made on the top far-side corner of the ball as the golfer sees it at address. Now, imagine what happens if the downswing becomes just a little more across the target line from out to in, and thus even steeper. The angle of attack becomes so acute that the clubhead cannot connect even with two-thirds of the ball, as happens in the normal slice. It's approach is so steep that it can contact, if anything, only the top half of the ball, or perhaps even only the top quarter of an inch. Result: a top — usually a top along the ground to the left.

From this, it should be clear that topping has little to do with your head, but is really the ultimate expression of a steep out-to-in, slicing-and-pulling swing pattern. That, in fact, is why the fault is so common among long and middle-handicap golfers, and so rare among good players.

The cure is equally obvious. To stop topping, you must stop slicing! You must, in fact, set yourself in such a position at address, and use the club in such a way, that you can swing into the back of the ball from behind and inside it, not over and down on it.

The second cause of topping is very much allied to the foregoing. Again it is largely a poor player's fault, but it also sometimes afflicts the competent golfer, because it can happen even when the set-up, swing arc and plane are good.

At address on every golf shot, the radius of the swing — the measurement from player to ball — is established by the unit of the left arm and the club, held in a more-or-less straight line. In the early part of the backswing this radius is maintained by the "one-piece" (no independent movements) combination of arm swing and shoulder turn. But at some point in the action, where we cock our wrists, the radius obviously decreases. If, then, in hitting the ball, the wrists do not uncock sufficiently to re-establish the radius of the swing at impact — re-establishing the left arm and club as a straight-line unit — the ball is likely to be topped, or at least hit "thin." Among fairly competent players this is the commonest cause of topping.

In the simplest terms, what basically causes both these "tops" — and also most thin or "bladed" shots — is too little use of the arms, hands and clubhead in the downswing. The inveterate slicer should understand that this problem is built into his game because of his steep downswing, which in turn emanates from his open clubface and out-to-in swing path. In the case of the better player, such lack of arm and wrist action arises usually from a deliberate attempt to "hit late." He would benefit from thinking of the downswing as a "re-measuring" — of getting his left arm and club back to the full radius of the address position before impact.

'Fat' shots start at address

Sclaffing is hitting the ground behind the ball, or hitting shots "fat." There are two common causes of this depressing disease.

Among both good and indifferent golfers alike, it can often be caused by nothing more complicated than bad posture at address, leading to loss of balance during the swing. The golfer stands to the ball in such a way — usually crouching or reaching for it — that his weight is pulled forward onto his toes. Inevitably the momentum of the downswing throws him even farther forward, with the result that he either "falls into" the shot, or is forced to dip his head and shoulders to get the clubhead to meet the ball. To avoid such a destructive fault is just one more reason why we must always start the swing from the correct set-up, remembering particularly in this case that the back must be reasonably straight.

The most common cause of sclaffing among reasonably accomplished golfers is poor co-ordination of body and hand action in the downswing. It is the opposite of the topper's problem — a tendency to hit **too** **early** with the hands and wrists, before the hips have cleared a way for them to swing past the body and out towards the target.

As most slicers are prone to topping, so most hookers are liable to sclaff occasional shots. What happens is that the sclaffer lengthens his swing radius by letting the clubhead catch up with and pass his hands before they have arrived back at the ball. In other words, the arc the clubhead is describing as it approaches impact is too wide — the hit is too "early" with the hands and arms. It is, indeed, to avoid catching the ground that ladies — most of whom must hit "early" to get the clubhead moving at maximum speed by impact — instinctively rise on their toes during the downswing.

For men golfers, however, the cure for this fault is definitely not to be found in ballet dancing. The sclaffer's basic problem is to better co-ordinate his downswing leg-hip movement with his arm and hand action — even to the point, for a time, of deliberately restricting his wrist action — deliberately hitting "later" with the hands and wrists.

125

HOW
-AND
WHAT-
TO
PRACTICE

I assume that the fact that you are reading this book means you want to improve at golf. I further assume that you want to improve badly enough to be prepared to give some time — even time that you would normally have spent playing — to practicing the game. Some of us are "naturally" more talented golfers than others, but **all** of us need to practice to develop and hold our full potential.

Over the past eight years I have spent a lot of my time operating and teaching at four Golf Centers. A main activity at these Centers is golf practice, so I know a fair amount about the habits of the average golfer in this direction. And what has come home to me is that he has a great deal to learn, not simply about the technicalities of golf, but about the sheer mechanics of practicing it. What seven out of 10 club golfers do when they go to a driving range, or down to the club with a bag of balls, may be exercise, but it isn't practice.

Let us start, therefore, by defining practice. It has three distinct forms.

The first and absolute primary form of practice you do at home sitting in an armchair, or driving the car to work. You do it with your brain, and it consists of thinking through the cause-and-effect of whatever you were doing the last time you played

golf. From here, still strictly on the mental plane, you decide through a logical reasoning process, not guesswork, exactly what you will be trying to achieve the next time you practice. Ideally, these thought processes should be based on lessons you have been taking from a professional in whom you have confidence. There is no substitute for personal tuition — for advice tailor-made for you as an individual. The vitally important thing, however, is never to practice until you have a clear picture of what you are trying to do.

The next form of practice is the physical execution of what you have planned mentally. This is swing-building and game-improving practice, and we will look at it in detail in a moment.

The third form of practice, which all good players do, and which I'd like to persuade you to do, is the prelude to any important round of golf. It isn't practice in the previous sense, because you are not trying to rebuild your game (or you shouldn't be). What you are trying to do, with anything from 10 to 50 shots, is to tune up the game you possess on that particular day; to loosen muscles, to get the "feel" of the clubs, to bring the clubface into the ball squarely and solidly and thereby boost your confidence for the ensuing round. And to find one workable swing "thought" for the day. This is the form of practice few club players bother to make the effort to do, but which is indispensable if you have serious golfing ambitions.

Having defined practice, let us now get back to the actual techniques of its swing-building form. (First, get hold of as many practice balls as you can, and throw out those that get badly cut or knocked about. They won't fly properly. And, if you want to enjoy your practice, and want your balls to last, keep them clean).

Once you get to the practice ground with cause, effect and treatment all clearly in mind, don't worry too much about where you hit the balls — especially if you are making a major swing change. Your fault will have been grooved, and the action incorporating it will probably feel comfortable. The cure might at first feel very strange, but you **must** persevere if a lasting improvement is to be made. If no improvement can be made over a reasonable period, re-think the problem or go back to your golf teacher.

Next, before you even draw a club from the bag, pick a definite point of aim. It doesn't matter what it is or how far away it is, so long as you can focus upon it easily.

Now, take out not your sand-iron nor your driver, but your six-iron. This club represents the mean average between the extremes of loft, shaft-length and power. It is the ideal swing-building club.

With the six-iron in your hand, the point of aim in your eye, and your swing objectives crystal clear in your mind, "break down the adhesions" with a few easy — but not careless — shots. Right from the outset try to grip correctly, aim the club as the first step in setting-up and set yourself correctly to that clubface alignment.

As you move into the session, try with every shot — **and I mean every single shot** — to do what your preliminary analysis has told you will give you a more solid strike or a straighter flight. Stick to your guns on this long enough to determine whether your mental assessment and cure was right. If it was, keep on practicing it only as long as you have plenty of mental and physical energy and enthusiasm. Then plant the relevant "feel" firmly in your mind for the next actual game you play.

My method of doing this sort of work — and it's *work* mentally and physically — would involve basically a six-iron, a hundred balls and as many 1-hour spells a week as I could manage. Even if I were a weekend player, I think I would be prepared to sacrifice actual playing time in order to make a lasting improvement. For instance, if I normally played twelve hours a week, I would play perhaps six and practice the other six.

If your assessment and cure are proved wrong after fair trial, do not give up, start experimenting at random, or lose your temper and pop off balls like a pom-pom gun. Take a rest. Go and sit down somewhere and think it all through sensibly again.

The flight of the ball tells you what you are doing, in your grip, in your swing-line relative to the target line, and in the angle at which your club is attacking the ball. **Use** this information at all times. Therein lies the only "secret" of golf.

A lot of resolution is necessary to carry through this kind of program, as it is to stick with any change in method when actually playing the course. Until the new system works, rounds played can be less than satisfying (which is a good reason for not playing too many!). If it is essential to try to play well on occasion while in the middle of changing your swing, obviously a compromise will have to be made.

I know only too well that weather and golf club facilities in Britain are against consistent and studied practice, but I am equally sure that if a golfer is keen enough he will find a means. (One of the reasons I got involved in building Golf Centers was to help him do so).

As a last resort he can erect a golf net at home. For years I used to smash golf balls into a net in my garage, and this is very valuable swing-changing practice, first because you haven't got a result to worry about, and secondly because there is no one to see how badly you are hitting the ball. If you are that keen but don't have the facilities to put up a net, try knocking lightweight plastic balls off an old doormat. Anything you can do to build up your golf muscles, to "groove" good actions, to keep swinging, must eventually pay dividends.

At the very worst, try every day to swing a club at home for a few minutes — concentrating on what you would be doing if you were hitting balls.

One more important point. I can understand the ordinary club golfer, who plays strictly for fun, fighting shy of the big ball. But to anyone who plays golf seriously, especially if he hopes to enter top-flight competition, I would say: you **must** practice (and play) with the American-sized ball.

The reason is quite simple. The U.S. 1.68-in. diameter ball, due to its greater susceptibility to sidespin, has to be struck more accurately than the British 1.62-in. ball to produce the same effect. The less accurately the bigger ball is hit, the less distance it will fly and the more it will hook or slice. Consequently, it shows up swing errors more acutely, and literally forces up the standard of the game — as has happened in America. On the other hand, once a golfer has developed a good enough technique to master the big ball, he will find it much easier to maneuver and "flight" than the 1.62-in. ball, and thereby he will gain much greater shot-making control than the golfer who plays only with the small ball.

Practicing for Tournaments

There is yet another type of practice — the kind one does on the course in preparing for a tournament. Many people go about it wrongly.

First and foremost, never play more than 27 holes a day in practice, especially the day before an event. It is essential to conserve both energy and enthusiasm for the actual competition. Very few world-class golfers ever play more than one round a day in practice.

Second, don't play sloppily in practice rounds. Try to hit the ball solidly, and don't be frightened of scoring well. A good practice round builds confidence.

Third, avoid if possible in serious practice a "four-ball with the boys." You are out there to study the course, to take note of its difficulties and dangers, to work out a plan of attack and defense. Competitive practice rounds are good, but if the game is too competitive or too social you are not likely to be as mentally alert as you should be.

Fourth, give yourself time to take note of the course and your own play. You need two or three extra balls handy to play extra shots, especially bunker shots, chips and putts, hitting them from where you think you will have to hit them on the big day. Take particular note of the clubs you play, especially if the weather is fair. In windy or wet conditions, of course, your practice round estimates may have to be revised.

Fifth, make a special note of the really punitive areas of the course — the two-shot penalty areas — and try to work out strategies to avoid them.

Sixth, although you may use your practice rounds to loosen up and make final swing adjustments, never fundamentally change your method during practice rounds. You are stuck with what you've brought with you. Try to make it work as best as possible.

GETTING CLUBS THAT FIT YOUR GAME

Club selection is a matter of prime importance from the moment you take up golf. The right clubs won't by themselves reduce your score, but the wrong clubs can most certainly inhibit your progress and pleasure, sometimes marginally, sometimes — if they are very wrong — drastically.

I believe no complete beginner need start the game by buying a full set of 14 clubs, the maximum permissible number. There are two reasons for this, neither of them financial. The first is that, until a golfer has gained enough ability to contact the ball squarely, he will not be able to make use of a high proportion of the clubs comprising a full set. In fact, some of them, like the driver and two-iron, will be definite liabilities. The second reason is that, not until he's been playing the game a while, can a golfer — or his professional — have any real concept of what clubs best suit him.

In my view what the beginner needs is half-a-dozen clubs, perhaps second-hand and certainly not too heavy, comprising ideally a three-wood, three-iron, five-iron, seven-iron, nine-iron, and a putter. Once he or she is underway, of course, the other clubs can be added as is convenient. Second-hand clubs are available from most good club professionals, and can sometimes be refurbished to look almost as good as new clubs.

A lot of golfers, when they step up the equipment ladder, go for what the trade calls a "second-line" model. These clubs are cheaper than the top-grade models, but are perfectly adequate if you are an occasional golfer, with no really serious competitive aspirations. They vary from the more expensive clubs mainly in the shaft. Top-quality golf club shafts — called by different names by different manufacturers, but virtually standard in composition — are highly scientific and subtle instruments, designed to cater to the swing tendencies and "feel" preferences of different players. Many club golfers get a psychological kick out of having the best shafts, but most could not actually tell the difference between top-quality shafts and cheaper ones in their shot-making.

What is really important in a golf club, once you are well past the raw novice stage, is the way the club feels when you swing it. This is determined largely by the weight of the head in relation to the weight of the other parts, and the flexibility of the shaft. No reliable system has yet been devised for defining club "feel" by formula, but an attempt is made through what is known as "swing-weight." This operates in the form of an alphabetical and numerical code, into the mysteries of which I won't go, except to say that D2 or D3 represents the norm for men's clubs, and that the lower a club's swing-weight designation, the lighter it should feel when swung, and the higher the number the heavier it should feel. (For example, C8 — the standard ladies' swing-weight — would feel light to most men, whereas E2 would feel almost impossibly heavy even to a professional.)

It is my conviction — and that of many playing and teaching professionals throughout the world today — that most ordinary golfers tend to use clubs that are too heavy for them; too heavy both in dead-weight and in swing-weight. One reason for this is that, in the hands of an eager or an inexperienced golfer, weight gives the impression of power. If he can feel a lot of mass in the clubhead, he senses that it will help him hit the ball a long way.

While a certain amount of weight is obviously essential to produce momentum, the most vital factors about the performance of golf clubs — which many golfers never realize or ignore — are speed and control. Given just enough weight in the clubhead, the distance the ball flies depends on the speed at which it is traveling at impact, plus the "squareness" of the hit. It is because they have become aware of this through long ex-perience that the majority of the world's top players now use light-headed drivers (speed) with stiffish shafts (control).

As a general principle, therefore, any golfer renewing his clubs should pay particular attention to their weight when actually swung. The lie and loft of the heads, the finish — and perhaps the player's name on the bottom — may be important to you. But the prime consideration should always be the dynamic — in motion — "feel" of the clubs. The type of grip and its thickness is a big factor here. Overall, you should have the sensation that you can swing the clubs fast, without undue effort, yet at the same time maintain control over them. If you err at all, err on the light side.

Golf is a highly individualistic game, which makes it impossible to fit clubs to broad groups of players. The chart on page 135, however, provides at least a guide to getting suitably equipped or re-equipped, in terms of shaft flex and swing-weight. It will be seen from this that there is a clear progression from one extreme of player to the other. Generalizing, it is that the less you play, or the less muscularly adept you are, or the older you are, the more flex you need in the shaft, and, correspondingly, the more clubhead "feel" you will get. Conversely, the more and better you play,

133

and the stronger and more agile you are, the less flex you will need in the shaft, and therefore the less clubhead "feel" you will get.

Maintaining Clubs

Keeping golf equipment in good condition isn't simply a matter of saving money and making the tools last. Well-maintained equipment is a great asset to your physical shot-making and your psychological outlook.

Iron clubheads should be kept clean, with all dirt removed from the grooves on the faces. These grooves help to impart backspin to the ball. If the grooves are full of dirt, the backspin will be minimized, thereby reducing your ball control. Iron clubs can most easily be cleaned by washing with a soapy solution or detergent. If you want to retain their polished finish, don't scrub them with abrasive, but give them an occasional treatment with metal polish.

Wooden clubheads need careful treatment if they are to retain both their effectiveness and their appearance. They should be protected at all times with head-covers — if they are not, the finish will soon be chipped by knocking against other clubs in the bag, and they will become more susceptible to warping through the affects of weather. Most important, never

leave wet covers on your woods. Dry the clubs when you have finished playing, and don't replace the covers until they, too, are perfectly dry. Leaving wet covers on woods is the greatest single cause of warped clubheads. Woods are best cleaned by wiping with a damp cloth, then polishing with a furniture preparation.

If you look at the clubs of the top professionals, you will find that, whatever the age or condition of the heads, the grips are always in excellent condition. This is because playing with dry, dirty, shiny and slippery grips makes an already difficult game even more problematical. If you use leather grips, they should occasionally be given a light application of glycerine, worked well into the leather and left to absorb overnight (clean very dirty grips with spirit first). If the grips have become very smooth, scraping the leather lightly with a metal edge will roughen them.

If you use rubber or composition grips, to prevent them becoming dry and slippery they need frequent washing with soap or detergent. If they are very worn and shiny, light sandpapering will often improve their condition.

It is worth remembering that, although clubs themselves can be made to last for years, grips have a limited life. I would say that a golfer who plays and practices a lot will need to replace his grips at least every two years, to get the best from himself. Any competent club professional will do the job, at little more than the cost of the grips themselves.

Remember, too, how important the feet are in golf, both during the swing itself and in enabling one to walk considerable distances in comfort without the legs tiring (a sure swing-wrecker). Golf shoe spikes wear down and become ineffective more quickly than most players imagine. Leather golf shoes should be carefully dried and cleaned, and if you want them to give the maximum service you should keep them on good shoe-trees, otherwise they will soon lose shape and comfort.

A GUIDE TO CLUB SELECTION		
Type of Golfer and/or Swing	Shaft	Swing-weight
Exceptionally muscular or powerful. Under 35. Very fast swing or hard hit. Excellent hand action.	X (extra-stiff)	D3-D5
Well-built, loose-limbed. Athletic. Under 40. Lively action. Fast swisher of the club.	X (extra stiff) or S (stiff)	D1-D4
Average build. Fit and active. Plenty of golf. Under 50. Medium-paced action. Reasonable clubhead speed. The "swinging-hit" player.	S	D0-D3
Slight build. Average strength. Sedentary life. Not a lot of golf. "Easy" action. Slow swing. "No hands." Lack of clubhead speed.	R (regular)	C9-D2
Small or slender. Not strong or agile in back, legs, arms and hands. Slow, restricted or very easy swing. Little hand action. Badly needs clubhead speed.	A (slightly whippier than R)	C8-D1
Senior golfers struggling to "stay with it"	A or L (ladies')	As for previous two categories depending on physique, health and golfing ability.

The foregoing is intended only as a guide. Obviously there must be exceptions to any rule. The best policy is to seek the advice of a knowledgeable and sympathetic professional. If he'll let you experiment with various types of club, so much the better.

135

2
PLAYING THE GAME

Your attitude is all-important

When I played in tournaments I tried:

1. Never to hit the ball until I had decided exactly what I was trying to do.

2. Never to attempt more than I could reasonably expect to achieve.

3. To try my utmost on every shot.

This advice is applicable to every golfer, whether he scores in the sixties or the hundreds: three thoughts to serve as a basic text in any keen golfer's approach to the game — something almost to write on the back of your glove or carry around the course on a prominent placard in your mind's eye. Let's look at the tenets individually.

Never hit the ball until you know what you are trying to do.

This really has two meanings. One obviously relates to summing up the shot in terms of distance, trajectory, ground and wind conditions, the lie of the ball, potential trouble areas, and so on. Thousands of golfers give insufficient attention to such matters. They simply grab a club and whale away almost blindly and wonder why, even when hitting the ball well, they never make a decent score.

Every golf hole and every golf shot requires **thought**. The better you can picture a given shot in your mind's eye, and the clearer your mind is about the shot you intend to play, the greater your chance of accomplishing it. Even that simple lesson alone would substantially lower many handicaps.

But there is more than assessing the shot in knowing what you are trying to do at golf. You want to know not only what the ball should do, but what you yourself are trying to do to get the ball to behave in that way. You need to know, consciously, what you are trying to do with your swing.

It doesn't matter whether it is a good swing, or an agricultural heave; if you have a single focal thought, you will have a better chance of making it work, not once in a while but repetitively. Repetition is the golden key to golf, and it usually starts with a repetitive thought pattern.

For a man like Ben Hogan, knowing what he is doing when he swings a golf club may well involve consciousness of the workings of a dozen different parts of the body, all welded together in a composite "feel." For Sam Snead it might be largely an instinctive, natural "feel." For the majority of golfers, the right way is somewhere between these two extremes. And the easiest manner in which they can focus their knowledge and swing ability is by the use of key thoughts, or gimmicks.

Before any important round I always hit a few balls, and the purpose of this is twofold: to loosen my muscles, and to decide upon my "swing thought" for the day. Every good player I've ever met follows this policy. (Joe Carr, the great Irish amateur, even used to write things like "Turn, you fool!" on his golf glove, where he could see it at address.) No matter how much in practice you may be or how "grooved" your action, the "feel," timing and "shape" of your swing will alter fractionally from day to day — even from round to round. It is vital, therefore, having discovered with a few preliminary shots or swings how your action is working, to decide upon a thought, a gimmick, that will keep it ticking over nicely.

The gimmick itself can take many different forms, depending on your ability and how you are playing at the time. It might be simply to ensure that your set-up — aim and stance — is right; a basic thought, as is the way the hands are gripping the club. It might be keeping your head still. It might be a push away of the club with the left side, or a slight drag back with the hands. You might think of not starting down to the ball until your left shoulder has gone under your chin — a "complete-the-back-swing" thought. You might concentrate on starting the down-swing by unwinding your hips.

The possibilities are endless.

Every player of accomplishment has a personal set of swing thoughts or gimmicks, which he will have discovered and proven effective in practice. If he is a thoughtful golfer, he will have indexed them in his mind in terms of cause and effect — "If I do this, that happens, and if I do that, this happens." In most cases the modifications will be very small — fine tuning. But such thoughts are vital to keeping a golf game in balance. The great thing is to find gimmicks that enable you to think quite clearly of what you are trying to do.

As an example, I might perhaps quote the Ryder Cup match of 1955 in America. I was nervous, and knew that in this condition I was apt to curtail my backswing. So for two whole days my ever-present swing thought was: "Don't start down until your left shoulder is opposite the ball." It helped me tremendously to concentrate, and I used it on every single full shot I played. Not once did I make a full swing without that thought in mind. And I played very well.

To derive maximum benefit from such gimmicks a clear understanding is necessary of what kinds of actions produce what kinds of shots, which is why the ambitious player must thoroughly understand the "ballistics" of the game — the flight characteristics of the ball when struck in a particular way.

A very useful thought for the good player is to remember how he finishes the swing when he's playing well, and to determine to finish that way on every full shot. Often this stops the common tendency — especially under pressure — to hit **at** the ball, rather than swinging the club **through** the ball.

There are scores of gimmicks of this kind. They all help you to "know what you are trying to do."

Play within your own limitations.

I've said this before, and I imagine I'll go on saying it until the cows come home: club golfers attempt things, not once but repeatedly, that the great players would never try. And it is this refusal to consider, let alone accept, their limitations — plus lack of technical knowledge of what is possible with a golf club and ball — that racks up the sevens, eights and nines on those sad scorecards.

I remember once drawing a prolonged groan from a St. Andrews gallery simply because I accepted my limitations. I'd started 70-71 in the Open Championship, and in my third round I put my second to the Road Hole right behind the notorious pot bunker to the left of the green. The shot seemed very difficult — chip the ball off a bare and sandy lie over the bunker and stop it near the pin, without going across the hard and narrow green onto the road. I weighed the situation very carefully, and the thought that kept coming to the forefront of my mind was: "Well, I can take five here, and still be in with a chance, but six or more would really upset me." So I played very conservatively onto the front of the green, a long way from the hole.

For this I was taken to task by about 5,000 Scots, most of whom, I imagine, would simply have waded in with the wedge before they'd had time to consider the little matter of percentages. I then holed the putt across the length of the green for a par. And — bless them all — then I was cheered!

As I've said, the shot was just about "on," but I was nervous and tense, and I doubted if I could bring it off. So I played within what I considered to be my own limitations. Even if I hadn't holed the putt, I'd still have had a safe five, whereas if I'd knocked the ball into the bunker or the road I could easily have had a major disaster.

If only average golfers would occasionally adopt the same policy! What a lot more cheerful faces there'd be in the bar!

One appreciates that a lot of the fun in the game for the club player lies in having a go, but surely the score counts too? If it does, a little more reality about one's own ability, and a little more assessment of the percentages, can work wonders. This does not presuppose a defensive attitude. By all means attack and have a go when there's a **reasonable** chance of success. But, when the thing is obviously impossible, accept your mistake and play to minimize its effect.

Playing the percentages, I might add, is not something you do only on recovery strokes. Innumerable times club golfers are faced with situations where some strategical thought, allied to common-sense assessment of their own capabilities, must result in an iron from the tee, or a sand-wedge instead of a four-iron from a fairway bunker, or a four-wood instead of a two-wood from the fairway. It might hurt your pride to accept the fact you **have** limitations, but it will rarely hurt your score.

Try your utmost on every shot

Easy to say, difficult to do. Yet this is one of the greatest factors in success or failure at golf. How many times have good players lost to poorer players simply because they didn't give maximum effort?

It is, of course, very easy to try on every shot on the first hole, and probably on the second and third holes, too. But what about the fifteenth and sixteenth holes, especially if things haven't been going well? There, often, is the acid test.

One of the things that annoys me most in golf is the people who say: "Well, of course, I only play for pleasure." I sometimes ask them how much pleasure they get out of having 120 smacks at it. Actually, I don't believe these people. I think they know that they'd get a lot more pleasure if they played better. Their attitude seems to me simply a lame excuse for dismal performance. After all, you've only got to compare the long handicapper's face and conversation when he's equalled or bettered his handicap and when he's taken a couple of hundred. He isn't the same man.

So, I say again, to get the maximum pleasure from your golf, try your hardest on every shot. This doesn't mean adopting the characteristics of a man contending for the Open, and taking 10 minutes to crawl around inspecting every blade of grass between you and the hole. It means above all, as I see it, concentrating on golf when you're playing golf, and conditioning yourself to the shot every time as you approach the ball. From there on, it is a question of thinking properly: forgetting the last shot, however it resulted, disregarding those to come, and focusing your attention exclusively on the shot at hand.

141

The very best example of trying on every shot I know is Jack Nicklaus. He carries it through even to the practice ground. He never rushes up and hits one quickly, or makes a sloppy swing. He makes a flat-out effort every time he approaches a golf ball. In practice he doesn't hit nearly as many balls as many top players do, but every one gets a 100 per cent try.

I found myself, when teaching heavily at Sandy Lodge a few years ago, that it is impossible to play golf well if you are not able to concentrate fully on your own game. Giving playing lessons in which most of my attention went to the pupil very quickly upset my golf. (Playing lessons are also — I might add — an ineffective way of teaching, in that the pupil has only one chance, and cannot really buckle down to eradicating a fault on the course as he can on a practice range.)

In Britain we have a national tendency to rate our golfing prowess in terms of the time it takes us to run through 18 holes. "Got round in two hours," we say, proudly, but we rarely mention the score. Possibly this is because we haven't got a score to mention — simply because we went around so fast we were unable to complete every hole. I am dead against slow play. But I am equally convinced that one of the factors behind America's golfing superiority is that almost every golfer in the U.S.A. plays every hole of every round to its full value. The American player, even at club level, says "I shot 94," and one knows that he did just that. We say "If I'd had fours at the ninth and the thirteenth, where I picked up, I'd have been round in 76." In short, we kid ourselves, and no one is more guilty of this than the middle-handicap player, with his "gimmes" and his reliance on his four-ball partner to win him the Sunday bet. Unfortunately, there is no doubt that if you are going to try to play the best golf of which you are capable, it is necessary to devote reasonable time and thought to each stroke, just as it is necessary to complete each hole.

What I am really suggesting is a maximum effort, and in this respect I would advise at least half-a-dozen warm-up shots and some putts before playing. The middle-handicapper is always in a hurry. He rushes to the club, into the locker-room, and out onto the course not having touched a club since the previous weekend. He then rushes into an appalling start, which sets the standard and the tempo for the rest of the round. No wonder his handicap stays high!

Mine would too if I tackled golf this way.

The art of competing

Michael Bonallack, five times British Amateur Champion, is the perfect example of what I would call a "mental golfer." Perhaps we could say, without being too uncomplimentary, that he is a maneuverer; a better competitor than striker. But, of course, that doesn't mean a hoot; the score counts. And when something clicks and he starts to strike the ball well, he wins everything.

And it is surprising, when you have a lot of knowledge, how something can click. One day you think :"Yes! That's it!" — and it is, for a period at least. This really is golf, keeping the swing "clicking." But to do this self-knowledge is essential. You must know your game inside out, as Michael does. Theoretical knowledge, applied to his own game, has been one of his greatest assets.

I see exactly the opposite approach so often as a teacher. People come to me and I get them hitting the ball well on the driving range. They are delighted, but often I am not, because I know that as soon as they go away and lose it they won't have a clue what to do to get it back again.

So many people can hit the ball beautifully only on the practice ground in front of a coach; so long as someone is there to hold their hand, tell them what to do. I think this is a form of lack of confidence, or, perhaps, of mental laziness. A teacher, however good, can only provide the framework. The player who wants to be really good must always work it out in detail for himself.

Bonallack's best asset, like a lot of great players, is his golfing brain. This isn't uncomplimentary. It has been true of Peter Thomson, Bobby Locke, Walter Hagen and many other great golfers. They were good strikers most of the time, perhaps, but their chief asset was a golfing brain which enabled them to overcome mechanical or technical deficiencies. In other words, they could nearly always score well when playing badly. They could **compete.**

I wish more people had this sort of golfing brain. There are no end of golfers who can hit the ball very well, professionals and amateurs alike, but there seem to be very few who can win championships. Those who do are the people who can think properly and keep their cool under heavy pressure.

All tournament players have been in the position many times of coming in after an event having played rubbish. With nine holes to go they have more or less given up mentally, and tended to play sloppily as a result. Then, once in, they have found they lost by a shot or two.

You always imagine that other people are doing far better than you are. Club golfers will have experienced the same thing.

This is a problem inherent in every form of competition where the action is spread out. The only answer is confidence in oneself, and a relentless determination to keep trying whatever happens. Peter Thomson is perhaps the supreme example of this type of temperament and he has won repeatedly as a result. Perhaps a "big head" helps; the sort of attitude that no one can do better than you in the long run. Mind you, there is no need to tell everyone that!

Just how do you score well when playing badly? Especially when you have been playing well and the collapse is sudden and shocking?

The most vital thing is to know what you can fall back on simply to move the ball from A to B. It doesn't matter what it is, or how the ball flies, so long as it will "repeat" and you have confidence in it.

For example, if Gary Player is at all worried about a shot, and has little margin for error, he knows that he can naturally draw the ball, and he will do just that. You might say that he mishits purposely, for the sake of the score. In other words, he has an absolutely reliable "tight" shot which comes to him easily, under any sort of pressure. I think this is the most important single piece of armament in a good golfer's arsenal. It doesn't matter if the shot is a slice, a hook, or even a half-top, so long as it is **repeatable;** so long as it can be played with confidence at any time.

Too many good golfers try too hard for technical perfection, and not hard enough to score well while striking poorly. Nobody ever hits every single shot perfectly. Even the finest strikers only hit six or seven shots in any one round exactly as they mean to. Many competent golfers find it difficult to accept this situation. They seek perfect striking and are unduly disappointed and disillusioned by their bad shots, which adversely affects their confidence and tenacity. It is impossible to achieve perfection of strike even on a practice ground, so how much more difficult must it be when the shots count; when one is playing under pressure?

If a Thomson or a Player went into a championship not hitting the ball well he would be what I'd call "sensibly perturbed." He would certainly be looking for "a way" in his mind and on the practice ground. But he would not be completely demoralized, because of his ability to **compete.** Whereas a lot of people in this position would be beaten before they even left the first tee. They would panic and become demoralized. The great competitor knows that he is a **pretty good striker,** which is all you need to be to win a great deal if you have the right mental attitude. If you haven't got the right mental attitude, you need to be a superlative striker to finish anywhere in the running. It would seem to me that the good competitor will go on winning almost irrespective of his striking, whereas the good striker who is a poor competitor is likely to shine only occasionally.

No golfer can play well unless he is keyed up. That doesn't mean he must walk onto the first tee trembling with fear, but he has to feel something, if only excitement, anticipation, the thrill of impending combat. Again, I think this is a question of being "sensibly perturbed," or calmly concerned. It is a feature of every good player. The Hogans, Palmers, Jacklins, whatever front they may present to the world, are keyed up every time it really matters. But perhaps the difference between them and lesser players is that they are in full control of their emotions. The tension in their case helps; in the lesser player, or the less experienced player, it breeds loss of control.

A bad start will quickly kill off the majority of golfers — sap both their confidence and their desire. I once asked one of the finest competitors in tour-

nament golf what his reaction would be to starting a major championship with a seven. He said: "I would just try to forget the seven and go on playing the other holes as they came. I certainly wouldn't be trying to make a sudden, dramatic recovery. I wouldn't think 'Now I've got to go 3-3-3,' or anything like that. You can never expect too much too fast. Over- anxiety to recoup a shot too often leads to loss of more. You have to wait for it, wait for the opportunities.

"I like to start off quietly. I don't believe in attacking right from the gun. On the first hole I never try to hit the drive very far. I simply try to get it into play somewhere. Then if I am left with say a six-iron to the green, I don't try to hammer it at the flag. I will be content simply to put it somewhere on the green. The same applies with putting. I'll be happy to get down in two. Once I've got the mood of the game and am getting into it, then I feel I can start attacking. But I think if you try to attack too early, you can run up fives and sixes very easily. You are trying too hard to get back the shots you've lost before you've really played yourself into reasonable form, let alone into an attacking position.

"Even when you have 'played yourself in,' there will be days when you are striking the shots well but the score won't come.

There is absolutely no percentage in getting distressed about it, as many golfers do. You can only go on trying to do your best and wait.

"The thing that irritates me most is playing a stupid shot, an ill-judged shot. I cannot excuse myself if I miss a shot through having not really thought about it. This is a lapse of concentration that shouldn't occur. I try never to make a stroke until I have decided quite definitely the type of shot I want to hit. It annoys me intensely if I play a stroke slackly, without these essential preliminaries. Generally the annoyance is increased by the cost of the error!"

It has to be admitted, of course, that everyone concentrates so much better when they are playing well. It is very difficult to do what is described above if things are going badly. Irritation undermines concentration, and you find that the bad shots, or rather the ill-judged shots, multiply. It is a vicious circle very difficult to break.

Naturally enough, many good competitors — Jacklin is a case in point — find it more difficult to concentrate in friendly games than in competition. The reason is because the player has not got himself on such a tight rein. When he is playing competitively he is steeled; he has thought himself into an every-effort attitude. This, I think, is why the first-class golfer finds it difficult to try hard in anything other than competitive rounds. He will tend to relax every time it doesn't really matter; in short, he can't be bothered when the pressure isn't on. It is a perfectly natural reaction, because the effort of concentration is one that cannot be maintained continuously. Thus the good player in practice rounds is often likely to hit poor shots. He hasn't yet put himself fully into a competitive frame of mind.

Whatever your level, however, remember that — with the right effort — you can almost always score better than you played.

The word for it is **competing.**

Specific strategies to cut your score

All of us, given fulfillment of a golfing wish, would choose to strike the ball well. Therein lies the game's greatest pleasure and satisfaction. But good striking alone does not produce good golf. Once we have learned to hit the ball well, our next problem is to learn how to score, how to "get around the course."

Golf, in fact, presents a dual problem. One is purely technical: the method of striking the ball. The other is tactical: the method of negotiating the course. Good striking of the ball, of course, is paramount to a first-class game. But it is not quality of striking alone that breeds champions. Champions are the people who can best apply this expertise to the strategical problems of course and climate, and to the tactical problems set by the infinitely varied form of golf holes. When they can continue to do this under the most acute pressure, they become world champions.

The average-to-poor golfer especially should think hard on this point. A variety of factors and circumstances — notably age and the demands of business — may put a limit upon how proficient he can make his striking method, because forging a swing is a matter of time, energy and physiology. But learning how to score makes no physical demands, nor does it require time beyond that already devoted to golf. What it requires above all is simply the application to one's game of the intelligence and common sense that are applied, automatically in most cases, to earning a living.

To me one of the fascinating aspects of this game is the speed with which an often highly intelligent individual's mental faculties desert him the moment he steps onto a golf course. It really is quite incredible how general this is.

We all suffer from this tendency to some degree, even the professional tournament golfer whose living depends on his clear-headedness just as much as his physical dexterity or his nervous stability. Often when I was not hitting the ball well in a tournament, my natural instinct was to let it affect my reason: to gamble, to physically force the thing to do my will, to go up to it and give it a quick, ignorant whack and have done. Yet, if I could control this temptation, often I would score better than I might have done when hitting the ball really well, simply because I was thinking properly and playing carefully within my capabilities at that moment.

Do not misunderstand me in this respect and assume I am suggesting a defensive attitude to golf. Every golfer must attack the course whenever the percentages are in his favor, subject to two factors: that he has realistically assessed those percentages, and that his scale of attack is within his own physical capabilities.

Really, if there is a short cut to lower scores, this is it. The road to better striking of the ball is a hard one, involving much study, practice and play. But if it is the score that matters most to you, a little more application to the tactical aspects of the game can bring notable results with little or no improvement in your striking ability.

Here are some specific examples:

147

Low-Handicap Players

1. Remember, on the first tee, that few top golfers attack the course in the first few holes. Play the opening holes within yourself and your handicap, whatever that may be. The first hole at Sandy Lodge is a par five. I know I can usually make par there; therefore, I aim to get a five, and sometimes end up making a birdie. But I never try to force a birdie out of this first hole. However, by the time I reach the 14th, also a par five, I am usually blasting away like mad in an effort to reach the green in two, looking for a birdie. The point I am making is that it is a good policy to play conservatively until you see how things are going.

2. Have you ever worked golf out this way? If you make four threes at the short holes, plus another three at a par-four hole, you can take five fives and still shoot 72 — so long as you don't take a six. At this level of play it is critical to make par at all the one-shotters, and never to go over par at any other hole by more than one stroke. If you can do that you will never be far away from "level fours." At the par-threes you are normally playing an iron shot from off a tee a known distance — everything is in your favor. At all other holes — especially the long, troublesome par-fours — you should plan your play so as

never to risk making more than five.

3. On most courses, the key to beating par for the very good player is the par-five holes. They are the easiest holes to birdie, and, once you're warmed up, they should be played as such, with a sense of attack; two big crashes to get there or thereabouts, then a lot of work to get down in only two more. Whatever you do on the rest of the course, don't play defensively on the fives unless there are some particularly dangerous aspects to the hole. Whack the ball for all you are worth and try to get "up." After all, the percentages are higher playing from a greenside bunker than from 120 yards out in the fairway. One word of warning, however: be very careful of the severe fairway cross-bunker, especially when it threatens the drive.

4. Don't improve the lie of the ball in winter, unless this is obligatory at your club. Sitting the ball up on a tuft every time leads to a sweeping action that can adversely affect your iron play. Playing the ball as it lies forces you to concentrate on accurate striking.

5. Never play a short shot — pitch, chip, putt — until you have decided in your mind's eye how the ball must react if it is to finish by the hole. Don't get stereotyped. Form a mental picture along the lines of "I want the ball to fly from here to there and roll from there to there." Then select the club that will do that for you most easily. And don't forget to allow for different levels. When chipping from below the level of the green, use a well-lofted club — nine-iron or wedge. Conversely, when you are chipping from above the green down to the putting surface, take a straighter-faced club than you normally would — a five-, six- or seven-iron. Why? In chipping from below the level of the green you are, in effect, decreasing the height of the shot. The ball does not drop so far, and will therefore run farther. From a level higher than the green, the loft of the club is increased by the ball falling farther. Consequently the ball will stop quicker.

6. If you are a poor bunker player — that is, if you can't get down in two pretty regularly from sand around the green — get out and practice bunker shots. Professional tournaments have shown us that green-side bunkers are no problem, and this is simply because the short sand shot is relatively easy given the right club, the right method and the right mental approach. Generally speaking, amateurs in this category are not as good as their handicaps from bunkers, simply because they've never practiced the shot and therefore lack confidence.

7. Unless ground conditions are very dry, hit your full seven-, eight- and nine-irons not at the hole but at the top of the flag. These are the scoring clubs. Use them as such. Most low handicap golfers are prone to under-club on approach shots. Instead of hitting, say, a controlled seven-iron at the stick, they thrash an eight-iron at the green. I find I tend to do this when I'm not playing well, but if I'm hitting the ball solidly I take ample club and fire straight at the top of the stick. Most low-handicap amateurs are often surprised at the clubs the best players use in approaching. Sam Snead, for instance, would often use a seven-iron where most club players would try to wallop an eight. You don't get prizes for distance with the pitching clubs. A controlled shot at the flag is always a much higher percentage shot than a big, swinging thrash in the general direction of the green. Incidentally, to get the best from the scoring clubs, it helps to know how far you hit the ball with your normal standard swing with each of them. I remember that Ben Hogan, at his best, knew within a couple of yards how far he would hit each iron under varying conditions. Normally there was a

149

12-yard variation on each club from the four-iron down, and when he practiced the caddie simply moved back that distance and the balls pitched at his feet. So, once you reach a good standard of striking, try to ascertain what each scoring club will do for you, and use this knowledge on the course.

8. Trust your swing. And concentrate on swinging through the ball. Many fairly good players don't improve because, when things go wrong, they stop striking and start steering. Fear makes them maneuver; undermines confidence in their method. Part of this is due to too great a consciousness of and concentration on hitting fairways and greens, instead of swinging the clubhead through the ball. Realize that the tighter or more difficult the shot, the more you must steel yourself to make a good pass: to swing the clubhead freely and fast.

9. If he's properly handicapped, the only time a scratch-to-six handicap golfer takes a viciously high score is when he loses control, not of his swing but of himself. This is true of all good players. They start badly, or have a disaster, get morose, angry, dispirited, and away goes the whole thing. Resolve now that this won't happen to you again. Decide to put yourself on a tight rein from the start of

every round, to take the rough with the smooth, and to keep trying whatever happens. If you can bring your thinking up to the level of your striking, you won't be over 80 very often.

Middle-Handicap Players

1. At this standard, "trouble" is generally the major score-wrecking factor. The player gets into it frequently and gets out of it successfully infrequently. For instance, few middle-handicap golfers in my experience can play even passably well from bunkers — many need an average of two shots to escape from sand. Thus, even a minimum of application to bunker play would probably reduce your score by three or more shots. The regular sand shot allows the biggest margin for error of any shot in golf. You can hit anywhere from half-an-inch to four inches behind the ball, and, so long as your technique is reasonably adequate, the ball will land on the green. Half the problem is that this grade of player becomes terrified as soon as he sees the ball drop into a bunker, because he doesn't have enough technical knowledge to be certain of getting out. Thus the best advice I can give to players of this grade is: (1) have a lesson on bunker shots, and (2) practice the basic technique of getting out of rough — the stuff you get into so often. Practicing from short rough will provide you with a clearer picture of how much to attempt, and the clubs and types of shot that will best succeed under varying conditions.

2. What is the first action in addressing a golf ball? Middle-handicap golfers rarely supply the right answer to that question, which is correct aiming of the clubface. Most first set themselves, then set the club down behind the ball, which means that the direction in which the clubface points is a matter of luck. You **must** first aim the clubface squarely at the target, then stand square to its alignment. The fact that very few players between 12 and 24 handicap do this is one of the major reasons why there are so many frustrated club golfers. They don't seem to realize that, unless the clubface is correctly aimed, even the perfectly struck shot will not finish on target.

3. Once you set foot on the golf course, **you have got to commit yourself to one thought during each swing.** The best way to find your "thought for the day" is to hit a few shots before you play. A lot of the time the pros are doing exactly that when they practice before a competitive round. There is nothing worse than cluttering and confusing your mind with too many technical thoughts prior to and

during the swing. But I believe that most golfers' concentration is helped by thinking of one specific thing, especially if this "peg for the day" has been developed while hitting a few pre-round "looseners."

4. Too many middle handicap golfers persist in using drivers that would put Arnold Palmer to the test. Not only are these clubs often too heavy, they are too straight-faced. Perhaps it is not generally realized that most golf clubs are designed on the assumption that the ball will be perfectly struck. Hence, unless you are a near-perfect striker, you may well benefit from certain modifications to your equipment. The driver is the major case in point. It is the most difficult club in the bag for the average golfer, and I am convinced that this is because it is too straight-faced. What the middle-handicapper needs for his tee-shot is a fairly deep-faced two-wood, a driver-size club with the loft of a brassie. Such a club would take an awful lot of the pain out of the average golfer's tee shot. The game would become physically easier for him, his drives would be longer and their direction less erratic. (If you do make this change, go for a light club, too).

5. Given reasonable competence from the tee, the middle-handicapper's greatest problem

151

is distance through the green. He is unable to equal the good player's long-iron shots. Here again the answer, as I see it, lies in equipment: specifically in a fairway wood that will supplant the two- and three-irons. As drivers in general are too straight-faced, so fairway woods for most average players are too deep-faced. A really shallow-faced wood, with four-wood or five-wood loft, might be the finest birthday present the club golfer could give himself. He would find it a great deal easier to play, especially from rough or poor lies, than the long irons, and repeated use would increase both his skill and his confidence on long approach shots. Another point on clubs: never be afraid to use fairway woods from the tee at par-three holes where the ball must fly all the way to the green to clear hazards — you have a far better chance of finishing in good shape than by mishitting a long iron. Tee the ball so that the center is level with the top of the clubface; and, if you want height, play the ball a little more forward than usual. Many Open championships have been won by golfers driving throughout with a two- or three-wood — even if it had a No. 1 written on the bottom! If your driver is "off," the little yardage you will lose by using a more-lofted wooden club will be more than offset by your increased control.

6. You will always play better golf when you think before you hit. This means approaching the course from a planned tactical, rather than a hit-and-hope, attitude. There is a way for every golfer to play every hole to maximum advantage. For example, if you are a slicer by nature and are playing a hole with a left-to-right wind and out of bounds on the right, do not stand up on the left-hand side of the tee and aim down the middle of the fairway. Stand on the right side of the tee and aim **away** from the trouble down the left-hand side of the fairway. This gives you the whole fairway to play with, instead of half of it if you aim down the middle. If there is a bunker at the point where your best drive will land, play a three-wood — or even an iron. Don't use a wood from rough when there is no hope of getting up with your second and you could get home easily with your third if you recovered with an iron. If you are playing poor iron shots, don't go for the pins — hit for the middle or "fat" of the greens and rely on your putter. If you have a pressure shot to play, get the ball from A to B your natural way, even if that is a slice or hook, rather than trying to play some good-looking or fancy stroke. Play the percentage shot every time.

7. Try to pick the club that will hit the ball pin-high. Playing with Bobby Locke years ago, I learned a great lesson about approach shots. I was hitting mine as straight as I ever have, right dead at the stick. But they were often short or strong. On this occasion, Locke's shots looked nowhere near as good. He was on the green, but left or right of the pin. Yet, when we came to putt, I was generally away. Locke's uncanny judgment of distance enabled him to hit the ball pin-high, even if he was a bit off-line. My directional accuracy was offset by errors in distance. I· was 20 feet short or beyond, while Locke's was 10 feet — possible birdie putts — to left or right.

8. Many middle-handicap players three-putt a lot. Why? They will tell you it's because they miss the short ones. It isn't, you know. It's because they don't knock the long ones close enough. On long and even middle-distance putts, practice rolling the ball up to **the vicinity of the hole.** Try to get it close, not in. The secret of "steady" putting — which is what every average player should primarily seek — is judgment of distance, not direction. How often one sees a long-handicapper spend five minutes minutely examining the line, only to knock a 15-yarder three yards past. Learn to roll that ball up to within a foot or two feet of the hole, and three-putting will very rarely be

one of your major problems.

9. Concentrate on your grip and your balance. The grip is the swing's steering wheel. Persevere in finding and keeping a hold on the club that allows you to apply the clubhead squarely to the ball at speed. Remember that it may not be the same for you as it is for Jack Nicklaus, or your friend Bert Bloggs; and remember, too, that a change of grip alters the alignment of the clubface at impact, for better or for worse. Try, too, to stay in balance throughout the shot. This basically is a question of footwork, and its mastery will be reflected in your scores. The golfer out of balance is generally applying his whole body to the ball. The well-balanced golfer is swinging the clubhead through the ball.

Long-Handicap Players
1. The poor player who is keen to improve needs above all else to take lessons. I would suggest that if his handicap is no better than 20 he needs a lesson a week for six weeks, plus as many practice sessions as he can manage between lessons. Although the majority of golfers seem to believe they can teach themselves, or that one fine day they'll suddenly happen upon "The Secret," I can assure them that there is no substitute for personal instruction and practice. Even if he has natural

ability, the beginner or poor golfer must channel it correctly. So many go on thrashing about in the dark, when a few hours with an instructor would light up their whole golfing lives.

2. When he has lessons, the poor player should insist that the instructor gives him no more than two specific things to do, and explains exactly why. The golfer must then concentrate exclusively on these, and ignore every piece of advice he may get elsewhere, no matter how well-informed its source may seem to be. The reason is simple. A great many golfers can spot what seems wrong with someone else's swing. Very few indeed can diagnose the root cause of the wrong; can hit on precisely what is necessary to put it right. Thus much of the amateur instruction given around golf clubs, no matter how well-intentioned it may be, serves only to confuse. Follow the advice of the specialist, whose job it is to simplify, and then stick to his simplifications.

3. Set your own par. For the 20-handicapper par is not 72 — it's 92. Most courses have four par-three holes, four par-five holes and 10 holes of varying lengths at which the scratchman's par is four. The tyro must reassess the figures printed on the card so that they come within his own capabilities. For instance, a long par-four will be a five for him — and if he gets a four he has, in effect, got a personal birdie. The same applies especially to difficult par-three holes; they become fours for the tyro.

4. Mix with and try to play with better golfers than yourself. Most good golfers are only too glad to encourage others to play the game well, and, once the ice is broken, can be of great help in doing so. This is not a question of learning to swing. It is more a question of learning scoring technique, strategy, tactics; when to pitch, when to chip, how to recover from trouble, when to play safe and when to attack, and so on. Careful observation of the good player in these areas can be very instructive — as, too, is the effect on one's own game of watching a good method and witnessing a good score.

5. Although the greatest pleasures in golf for most people derive from the long game, it is possible to improve your scores drastically by concentrating exclusively on the short game. In fact, this is the quickest and easiest way for the poor player to improve. It may not be particularly satisfying, but at least it engenders a reasonable playing level; and practice in the short game has the advantage of teaching control and "feel" that must help your long game, too. So if your interest is in scoring above all else, work at that short game as hard as you can.

6. Don't be frightened to take a putter from off the green, if circumstances make a lofted shot more difficult. Obviously, if the grass is thick on fairway or apron, or the ground is broken or muddy, the percentages are with a *slightly* lofted shot. If the ground is smooth and clean, by all means use a putter. Tournament pros know that a bad putt will almost always finish better than a bad chip, under these conditions. So should you.

7. It is obviously as wrong never to "have a go" as it is to play every hole aggressively. You must strike a balance, as with most things in life. Yet, too often I find myself — at my most caustic — saying to someone "Who do you think you are, Jack Nicklaus?" I say it, meaning to provoke, when I see players with very little ability attempting absolutely impossible shots. I never cease to be amazed at the optimism of so many club golfers. They are always expecting to hit the shot of a lifetime.

8. A valuable avenue to improvement, both in method and in scoring tactics, is through studying professionals in tournament play. Indeed, I believe this is essential if one is ever to become a really first-class golfer. Certainly if my son wants to come into golf I shall make sure that he watches good golfers at an early age. Watching first-class play is one of the best ways I know of developing the right attitudes and methods to both the swing and the tricks of scoring.

9. You can't pay too much attention to the grip and the set-up. They are fundamental to good golf. Once you've got them passably right, think primarily of swinging your arms. A vast amount is written and talked about almost every part of the anatomy in relation to the golf swing, with the notable exception of the arms. Yet, they do the *swinging*. From a good set-up, if you clear your right side (pivot correctly), while swinging your arms **up and in,** then clear your left side while swinging your arms **down** in the downswing, you won't be far away from a decent game. Remember, if your arms swing, your wrists and hands will automatically apply the clubhead to the ball — and that is your overriding objective.

Beating the weather

Brute strength and blind fury will achieve even less in bad weather than in perfect playing conditions. When you are cold, stiff-muscled, or restricted by clothing, any effort to smash the cover off the ball leads generally to an even greater loss of control. To know not only what you are trying to do, but what you are capable of doing, is always a help at golf. In rough weather it is essential. You must be prepared to play more conservatively, and when a birdie does come along, slip it onto your score as a pleasant surprise rather than an anticipated bonus.

Do not force the long par fours and fives. Accept the fact that in winter a long par-four may become a par-five, and a reachable five in summer a much more difficult five. Give yourself plenty of club, and accept the conditions as you find them. Never try to bash the ball into submission. The quickest way to fall flat on your face in bad weather is to try to tear the course apart.

The chief technical problem in wet conditions is to strike the ball squarely and cleanly. Water, mud and long wet grass combine against you to make this extremely difficult. Consequently, it is worth sacrificing a little distance in favor of a more solid strike. Think "Strike it flush," not "Hit it far." Quiet your game down, if necessary, in order to swing the clubface squarely into the back of the ball.

Generally in bad weather or ground conditions you should use more loft than you would normally. You need to get a wet ball flying, so don't overdo the straight-faced clubs. The four- and five-woods can effectively replace the two- three- and four-irons, especially among poorer players. These lofted woods will move the ball well even from wet rough, and are a boon for long shots from soggy or "shaggy" fairways.

Possibly the worst of all rough weather problems is wind. This is really what plays havoc with our enjoyment and our scores.

The answer, again, is to keep your head; to accept the added difficulties and to counter them by playing within yourself. The wind should be used rather than fought. When you are playing against it, take plenty of club, **really** over-club, shorten and slow down your backswing, keep your feet on the ground, and endeavor to swing the clubhead not **at** but **through** the ball.

Too many golfers, even good ones, cannot make themselves punch say a low five-iron when the distance in normal conditions would require a seven-iron. They would rather gamble on hitting a "miracle" seven-iron. Ninety-nine times out of a hundred such a shot will be blown away, but these stalwarts never learn. They seem to feel that they can allow themselves to attempt only the shots they regard as "proper golf shots." I can assure them that **any** shot arriving on target, no matter how it got there, is an excellent golf shot in a pro's book.

Downwind the ball will fly farther, so long as you give it plenty of air. Adjust your club selection accordingly. Very often, in a strong backwind, a three-wood from the tee will go farther through the air than a driver, but will stop quicker. Make use of this sort of knowledge when the conditions are against you.

High crosswinds are everybody's nightmare, but, again, they can be used rather than fought. My tactics vary according to the distance of the shot and the degree of accuracy needed. In a big right-to-left wind, I would aim off to the right on the tee and let the wind bring the ball back to center fairway. In the same wind on an approach shot I would probably try to cut the ball into the wind, hold it up by shaping it into the wind, because a with-the-wind hooked shot is difficult to control when the target is small.

This, of course, demands a high level of ball control, which many golfers don't pretend to possess. Even so, they must decide how their standard shot is likely to be affected by wind, and make an appropriate allowance in aim.

The essential thing is to decide very clearly what you are trying to do **before** you actually attempt it.

Tournament golf—an insight

Depending on a person's temperament and outlook, the life of the professional tournament golfer seems to him either utopia or hell. Either way, just what goes on behind the scenes and within the mind of a man playing golf for a living might be of some interest to the thousands who play just for fun. Some years ago, in a mellow mood, I was persuaded to "think aloud" about my life as a tournament player.

Here's how it came out:

I wake up. I am at a tournament and it is a practice day. A practice day! Before I'm properly awake I'm happy. My first conscious thought is one of delight. I love practice days. I shall be out playing golf, on a fine course, with nothing much at stake, with people I like, people who are just as good, usually better, than me. I shall be trying very hard, as hard as in the tournament proper. We shall have a small gamble, not much, with an agreement about hitting extra shots so that we can get the feel of the course.

They are great fun, the practice days. I look forward to them all winter. The thought of them, perhaps as much as the tournaments, makes me keen after the winter. For years now I have played little golf from September to April. I have taught hard all winter. Golf, the start of the season, is almost a holiday for me. I really get wound up about it. I think about my game, practice, plan the circuit. It is invigorating and exciting.

At tournaments I hit as many balls as anyone. They say, generally rightly, that if you haven't brought it with you, you won't find it there. But usually I hit golf balls because I really enjoy hitting them — especially when there is someone to pick them up. I delight in all the aspects of practice, the sessions on the practice ground, the pre-tournament rounds, the evening putting for small stakes.

Some practice sessions are better than others. The facilities available make a big difference. We are sometimes accused of wearing our bottoms flat in hotel lounges, but many tournament practice facilities are poor to downright bad. When they are good, they are well used, although perhaps not as much as they should be. I'm sure proper facilities would increase practice, and eventually playing standards. This is so true of America. The practice facilities there are superb. This encourages players to work at their games, gives them every chance. Over here, so often, practice is a problem. You have to work at finding the facilities before you can work at your game.

I'm sure that tournaments appeal to me because it is so wonderful just to have my own golf to worry about. As a teacher, I spend most of my time and energy on other people's problems. A day without them is a free day — a day to really enjoy.

On the first day of the tournament I wake up and my first thought is that this is not going to be as nice a day as yesterday. But there is a thrill about it — butterflies in the stomach that get you out of bed, especially if you've played well in practice and like the course, and things — things like starting times and caddies — are going well. At this stage you are in the hunt. Everyone is in the hunt. There is a thrill-of-the-chase feeling. If you love competing, as I do, it is exciting.

But as you shave and dress, guessing at the weather, and go about the business of getting ready from a suitcase, the excitement alternates with other feelings. A nervy sort of anticipation. Anxiety. Dread, even. It is so easy to let your mind draw pictures. Too often they are not of long putts holed, of drives splitting the fairway.

I am a bit of a worrier, a bit of a fidget, I suppose. You can't help being a little on edge. Sometimes silly things irritate me easily, people's conversation, the service at breakfast, what the papers say. Silly things. I try not to show it, but quite often it's there. Everything sometimes seems extraordinarily clear and sharp to me. I suppose one is in a hurry to get on with it, and life sometimes reacts against you.

There is a routine to be gone through. Drive to the course, get the clubs, meet the caddie, change, hit the practice shots, putt. It induces a sort of preoccupation. People talk to me, but sometimes what they say doesn't register. Sometimes it registers too clearly!

However often you do it, you never quite get really blasé about it, nor about the first tee. We can all put on the act — relaxation, nonchalance. Inside we burn, a lot or a little, depending on our temperament. And this is right and proper. It would not be good not to be keyed up. The problem is to strike a balance between being nicely keyed up and . . . what? — those other feelings.

So much depends on the event, if it is a "routine" one, a big one, or a really big one. And on the golf course. And on how much in contention you know yourself to be.

Generally my feelings on the first tee depend on the difficulty of the drive. If it is really tough, I feel very conscious of the fact in the first round of a big tournament. Something I have only just realized is that very often I play far too defensively in first rounds, starting with the first drive. I can so easily start "steering" from the word go. I would like to make myself play from the off as I generally do in the third and fourth rounds, but there is a good reason why often I don't: qualifying. We are all acutely conscious of this at times, this need to qualify, to miss the half-way "cut." It can do odd things to your swing if you let it.

The devil of qualifying is that you often don't know what you've got to do. Sometimes you play on the last day if you are 10 shots off the leader's pace at half-way. At other times you can be seven shots too many and start for home after two rounds.

Starting times can make a big difference to your mood. Personally, I always prefer a morning time. You can look out of the window then and know what the weather's doing, and adjust yourself to it. You haven't got time to kill, eking out the minutes somehow, wondering if

159

the gale or the rain is coming up just for you.

I can't hurry on the day of a tournament. I can't dress or shave or drive quickly. I want plenty of time for whatever I've got to do. I like to arrive at the club about 75 minutes before I go out. I hit balls for perhaps 30 minutes, putt for 15 minutes. It can take me five minutes to put my shoes on, but I'm always ready 15 minutes before my starting time.

I try to plan the course. Where I have to be careful. Where I can attack. The day tells you whether the scores are going to be high or low. The practice ground gives you an idea of your own likely score. I bring all these things into the reckoning before I go out. I like to know specifically what I am trying to do. I can't go out and just hit it around in a vague sort of way, and let the score come or go as it will. I need a plan, a target, a definite objective.

I have learned to tackle tournaments in this fashion the hard way. Sometimes in the past I've become discouraged after a few holes, and, without a definite sort of mental schedule, have let it go, only to find that if I'd kept plugging along I'd have been O.K. The one thing you've really got to learn is never to give up. If you can make a realistic reckoning of how the scoring is likely to go, according to the course and con-

ditions, you're less likely to become either too disheartened or too elated.

I never eat much at a tournament. I have a large evening meal, a convivial meal with friends when possible, but very little breakfast or lunch. I drink as much as usual, which is never a lot. I'll have two or three whiskies in the evening, perhaps a beer or gin and tonic after the round if I've played in the morning. I've tried not drinking, dieting, drinking milk, and so on, but they've made no difference at all. I've reached the conclusion that if you are a fairly normal sort of being, the answer is to stay that way.

On the course in tournaments, I'm not aware of my nerves twanging more than most, but afterwards, back in the locker-room, you realize how much you've taken out of yourself. Often I feel very tired, both physically and mentally. Usually I am either depressed or quietly elated, depending on my score and how I've hit the ball.

How you actually hit the ball makes a big difference, whatever the score. A 68 will please you if you've not played very well, but at the same time it is worrying, because there is the next round. If you follow up with 74 or more, "He's cracked," they say.

If I've been playing in the morning, and playing well, in the afternoon I often sleep. I can always sleep after lunch if my game's reasonable. If I'm hitting the ball badly I often go out and practice in the afternoon. If it is a lovely day, often I just go and watch golf. Sitting behind a green somewhere.

In the evening we eat, well and leisurely when possible, go to the movies, have a drink or two, play cards, talk — it varies.

What do we talk about? Golf — and . . . what do men talk about? But our golf talk isn't shot-by-shot stuff. The first thing you have to learn if you want to keep your friends in the tournament game is not to tell other people about your round. This really is out.

We talk golf in a general way. We laugh a lot about it. You can always tell stories against yourself and raise a laugh. Often, especially among men like Thomson, Alliss, Hunt, Thomas, the talk is serious. We get really deep on a wide range of subjects. Our golf talk is general and diversified — technique, theory, tournament organization, golf politics and personalities, and so on.

Funnily enough, we do not talk in a selfish way. We don't complain about our lot, nor are we "catty." I think our talk is generally amiable and constructive.

On the second day of a tournament the first thing I think about when I wake up is what I did yesterday. If you've made a good first-day score, there really is a thrill about the second day, a zest to get out onto the course and do another one. If the first round wasn't so good, there's the challenge of trying to improve. I find, whichever way it may be, that my state of mind on the second day is totally different from the first. In fact, it would be good for me to be able to start a tournament in the frame of mind I'm normally in on the second day.

The way I'm striking the ball affects me very much. My mood almost entirely depends on this once a tournament has begun. The trouble is that I know only too well just how I am hitting the ball. I can't kid myself. If I'm striking well, my confidence is high. If I'm not hitting the ball flush, my confidence is at a low level. I am full of trepidation about how and where I'm going to hit it. The putting doesn't trouble me too much if I'm playing badly. But if my long game's good, I immediately feel extra pressure on my putting — it really is the difference between success and failure when you are playing well. This very knowledge doesn't help.

On the second day there is almost the same sense of urgency about life as there was on the first. You want to get at it, either to consolidate or recoup. After this half-way stage there is a greater feeling of relaxation. Either you've qualified or you've

161

packed and gone home.

I go home immediately if I haven't qualified — from the course into the car and away as fast as I can. I cannot bear to hang around at a place where I've failed.

But if you've qualified, the last day is tremendous fun. Now you can try as hard as possible with few fears or phobias. All I can do now is win or lose, make a high place or a low one. Somehow I am more relaxed, my whole game is more free and easy.

Even in this happy position, however, if I get into a winning position, the pressure bears down and causes me sometimes to start playing defensively. Defensive play at the critical juncture has always been my chief obstacle (and I don't have a corner on it!).

I think recently I have become more philosophic about the game. I try to think, "Well, here I am, needing a four to win," or qualify or whatever, and I say to myself that all I can do is my best. You can do no more in golf. Sometimes when you hit the ball perfectly it fails to work for you. At other times you mishit it and you get a lucky break. All you can give any shot is your best try. If you fail then, you just aren't good enough — or, if you prefer it, your luck isn't!

My thoughts on the journey home after a tournament naturally depend on how I've performed. If I have not played well, but with no major disasters, I think about my game, my swing, about why I am hitting the ball badly, and when I get home I cannot wait to get out to practice and to put it right. Sometimes, though, one finishes poorly despite having played well, perhaps because of one or two major disasters. If this is the case I am already, as I'm on my way home, looking forward to the next tournament. If I finish in from fifth to tenth place I generally drive home thinking mainly about where I dropped the vital shots.

I play every round, every stroke, again on the way home. If I have finished high I am very elated. But whichever way it has gone, I always have some very definite feelings!

I shall be so much sadder when I feel that my competitive days are over.

N.B. Now my competitive days *are* over, I'm pleased to report that I'm **not** sadder at all. I smile at myself now — how success in golf tournaments was so important to me. Now I am just grateful to be able to earn a living in a game I love so much. For me, I suppose, the challenge of tournament golf has been replaced by the challenge of trying to bring pleasurable golf to "the masses" at a price they can afford.

3
MORE PRACTICAL GOLF

Read the books—but forget the cliches

"Now, what seems to be your trouble?"

"Well, to begin with I just don't seem to be able to get any real distance with my woods. And then, on top of that, I can rarely get a long-iron off the ground, and if I do I usually slice it. And then somehow there doesn't seem to be any crispness in my shots any more . . ."

"All right, let's see you hit a couple."

So off he goes. He grips the club quite well and has basically the sort of set-up that will allow him to take the club away from the ball and bring it back on the right path and plane. The actual shape of his swing is fairly good. Obviously here is a golfer who knows quite a bit about it, has worked at it, and is very keen to play well. But he isn't playing well. For some reason — although what I call the static basics are right and his swing is passable — even his good shots are weak, lacking in authority. Why? Where is he going wrong?

As almost always in my teaching, I start by asking him where **he** thinks he's going wrong. And right away we get to the heart of the problem.

"Well," he says, "I've been reading some golf books lately, and looking at pictures of the top players, and I've got the feeling that I've been hitting the ball too early — hitting from the top. Most of these good players say that you've got to delay your hand action right to the last second, and you can see how they do that in those wonderful pictures half-way through the downswing. So I felt that if I were able to get a little bit more of that into my swing — hit it later — I'd probably improve quite a lot."

Oh, Mr. Golfer! What heart-aches you do give yourself!

Here is a man who ought to play quite well and enjoyably. Instead, he is standing before me in a state of controlled desperation, imploring help and prepared to go to the ends of the earth to find it. And yet his difficulty is so simple and so quickly curable as to be almost laughable. What is he doing wrong? Just one thing: trying **not** to hit the ball! Trying to hit it "late," and thereby guaranteeing that he hardly hits it at all.

Our golfer's problem is one of the commonest I and all my assistants at the golf centers are confronted with each day. Among all the passably good and even the very good players who come to us, a deliberate effort to "hit late" is one of the biggest single faults. What's worse, it is on the increase!

It is easy to understand why. The beginning golfer has little or no knowledge of theoretical

166

technique, and his natural instinct is to have a good, uninhibited swish at the ball. Only as a person begins to comprehend the need for control in golf does he lose the hit-it-hard-with-everything instinct. Sooner or later he learns that if the ball is to behave more or less as he requires it to, certain rules of method must govern the manner by which it is struck. This is the first inhibiting factor in actually hitting the ball, but it is an essential one, because golf is no game at all without some sort of control.

It is the next stage that does the real damage. Ever more eager to improve, the golfer seeks more and more knowledge about the theory of technique. If in search of it he simply goes to a competent professional, he will rarely damage his prospects, because the learning will be a direct physical process, rather than an abstract mental one — he will learn what he himself as an individual needs to know, personally, simply and directly.

But few keen players are prepared to stop at that point. Golf is a game of continual searching, and, even if a player has been well taught, he often has a natural and sometimes irresistible urge for further private exploration, especially of the more intricate mysteries of "method." Invariably, this leads to an increasing study of instructional literature, in magazines and especially in books carrying the signatures of the top tournament players.

And there is the crunch. Within these pages are depicted the swings of the world's great golfers, stopped at every compasspoint by the marvels of modern photography. And the most fascinating picture of all, sooner or later, is the one half-way through the downswing, the one showing the hands almost opposite the ball and the clubhead still somewhere up around the right shoulder — the "late hit."

Combined with the illustrious author's comments about how important delayed hand and wrist action is to his own game, these pictures bring a heady message to the aspiring golfer. Frequently he will come to see in them the key to golfing utopia.

He couldn't be more wrong! And to show you why, I'd like you to think very carefully about the following four points:

1. Until the development of the high-speed camera, the phrase "late-hit" was unknown in golf's vocabulary. None of the early masters of the game referred to it — or anything like it — in their books or teaching.

2. The speed of human reaction — the response of muscles to the brain's command — is such that any deliberate attempt to "hit late," to hold back the club artificially until a certain

moment, must inhibit a true swinging motion. The golf swing takes place too quickly for the average golfer to be able consciously to time a "late hit." Thus, the "late hit" — if it is there at all — must be a **reflex action;** the result of other actions and inter-actions, a natural segment of a whole movement, not an artificial or contrived action of the mind and muscle outside the spontaneous flow of the golf swing. If this is so — and it is scientifically provable — any deliberate effort to "hit late" will have the opposite effect to the one intended, i.e., it will **inhibit** the speed of the clubhead rather than increase it.

There are no set positions in golf, whatever those lovely photographs may appear to show. You swing through 10 or 10 million positions, depending on whether you use a cheap camera or an expensive one.

3. The majority of authors of golf books and instructional articles have superb natural and subconscious hand and wrist action. They have obtained it usually by starting the game very young and playing intensively as children, then by practicing and playing golf daily all their lives. The strength and coordination this breeds over a long period means that the problem for most fine players is to control the hit in some way, because it causes them to hook.

Their hands and wrists are so strong and "lively" as to become shot-wreckers if they work independently of the body action. Hence, the feeling of the good player is often that he must delay the hit through his hands, wrists and arms. He doesn't actually do so, the "late hit" one sees in photographs being caused more by his overall body action than by a deliberate inhibition of his arms, hands or wrists. But a sense of delaying the "release" of hands and wrists is often the **feeling** he has, as a result of his lifelong work at the game.

Golf books written by great players rarely state that the author posessed 80 per cent of his game — his "engine" — without knowing it. They are generally concerned with what he feels or thinks he is doing in finding the other 20 per cent of his game, by tuning this "engine," by positioning and "grooving" his natural power. And, because it is easier to become repetitive by controlling body action than it is by wrist and hand action — **once one has the "engine"** — the good player will be concerned above all with his body action.

To write in this manner is, of course, in no way dishonest from the great player's standpoint. What he says is valid for the person who possesses a comparable amount of natural ability at the outset. The flaw for most golfers lies in the assumption that they have the ability — that they have the "engine." If they haven't — and most haven't — the author is starting too far down the road for them.

It is for this reason that I believe books by top players should be entitled "How *I* Play Golf," as opposed to "How *To* Play Golf." I often feel that a few great golfers, who mostly fear a hook on virtually every full shot they play, are preaching anti-hook techniques to a world of born slicers. And it will keep me in business as a golf teacher for ever!

4. Most average club golfers — even the very good club golfers — do not, if they work at something other than golf for a living and are not usually physically gifted, have either the muscular or co-ordinative qualities to employ **any** inhibiting factors in the swing. As I stressed in the previous chapter, their problem is to generate more clubhead speed, not to cut it down. They need to get all the "swish" they can into their shots; to eliminate from the swing anything that will reduce the full, free flow of the clubhead into the ball. Obviously they will then have to learn to control this speed, but the chief and first problem is actually to acquire it. For the vast majority of people, **any deliberate attempt to "hit late" will definitely reduce the speed at which the clubhead meets the ball,** and therefore both the distance the ball flies and the "authority" of the shot.

Thus, there are very few golfers in the world who should try to cure their faults by slowing down the clubhead. Instead, the average player usually needs to feel (especially if he has been consciously trying to "hit late") that he is moving the clubhead as fast as possible towards the back of the ball from the top of his swing; that he is trying to generate maximum clubhead speed with his *arms,* for if they work his hands and wrists will surely apply the club to the ball.

If the golfer had Ben Hogan's arms and hands, Arnold Palmer's back and Jack Nicklaus's legs, his problem would be to hold back his clubhead until his body had positioned him in such a way that he could apply it correctly and repetitively. But the average golfer has none of these attributes; so, in trying to hit a golf ball hard and far, instinctively he tends to swing himself instead of using himself to swing the club. Shoulders whirl, head wobbles, legs collapse. He uses everything **except** the clubhead, and by so doing both slows down the clubhead and throws it badly off line.

The average golfer who tends to slice the long shots has not to hit later, but **to hit earlier with the clubhead.** He has to find a way to produce maximum clubhead speed through his arms, wrists and hands without destructive interference from his shoulders. Above all, he needs to learn to swing the clubhead with freedom, with abandon almost, and to eliminate from his mind all thoughts of "contriving" a contact; of having to maneuver the swing artificially to get the clubhead away from or back to the ball.

The first step in so doing is certainly to give up any conscious notion of "late hitting," and to determine once and for all to let the club *swing* freely, fluidly and as fast as possible.

While we're about it, let's punch holes in a few more of some prime "book" cliches:

"Keep Your Head Down"

I should think 25 per cent of people who are making golf very much more difficult for themselves than it need be are doing so as the result of the time-honored expression "Keep your head down." In fact, I have a saying that I find myself trotting out more and more often when teaching: "Keep your head down like that and you will keep me in business forever." The recipient is usually the pupil who stands there with chin firmly jammed into his chest, back of neck parallel to the floor, knees straight, and legs pressed back rigid as gateposts.

Thousands do this; in fact,

keeping the head down too long is as common an error in my teaching experience as bringing it up (or, rather, having it forced up) too quickly. And the effects are likely to be even more disastrous, because, if the head is forced to stay down too long, it becomes impossible to unwind the body correctly, thus inhibiting the free swing through of the clubhead. So never on full shots make a deliberate attempt to keep your head down. Simply try to keep it reasonably still until the ball has been hit, then let it go freely wherever it wants.

To play golf well it is helpful if the head does not move vertically or laterally to any great degree until the ball has been hit. But this does not mean that the head must be held in a fixed and rigid position. It means that the swing has to be executed in such a way that the head **automatically** remains in roughly the same place until the sweep of the club, arms and body naturally pulls it around and up.

I believe that, apart from short shots where anxiety plays a part, golfers rarely if ever lift their heads involuntarily, and certainly never consciously. The **natural** thing to do is look at the ball until it has been hit, which is what most people would normally do, **were there not something in their swing which causes, even forces, the head to move before it should.** In other words, "head up" is the EFFECT of an error in the swing, not, as so many believe, the CAUSE in itself of a bad swing.

Remember that good golf begins at ground level. The stance has a tremendous amount to do with "head up." For instance, if you start with straight legs and a rounded back, you are more than half-way to having your head forced out of position. A solid stance is essential because it makes for a good upper body turn, which is a major key to good golf. I would go so far as to say that every time you "lift your head" you are setting your upper body incorrectly at address, or using it wrongly in the swing.

A good set-up — aim and posture — will enable you to position your head and neck where they can comfortably stay *relatively* still until after the ball is hit. A bad set-up will create errors in body movement that force the head to move. For example, the lesser player is always apt to try to hit the ball with his body, which causes him to move his head to the left in the downswing — one of the most common causes of the cry "head up" from his friends.

Another shot-wrecking tendency of the average player is to move his head upwards on the backswing, instead of turning his shoulders round the axis of his spine. The good player's head may dip a little at impact as the hit comes in, but it will never move upwards as he comes into the ball — a frequent error of high handicappers with a tendency to stoop over the ball at address.

Some teachers maintain that moving the head is less important than "looking at the ball," but looking at the ball can also be overdone. Few of the great players are conscious of actually seeing the ball hit on full shots. They look at and "see" the ball, but they do not focus or register sharply upon it. The attention of the eyes is held by the ball in a general, rather than a pin-pointed or concentrated, sense. Too much consciousness of the ball can take all rhythm out of the swing. Indeed, it is virtually impossible, once you start to move, to concentrate specifically on looking at the ball. There is a consciousness of it, but rarely more.

Too many people who are not good enough *swingers* are glaring down at a divot mark when the unwind of the *swing* should have carried them through to a position where they can watch the ball sailing to the green. Never let "head down" or "look at the ball' curtail the freedom and fluidity of your swing.

When I tell you that, even at 46, I would confidently play any six-handicap player blindfolded so long as I could look at the ball as I addressed it, and on the greens, it might help you to believe that the head is not so vital as the cliches suggest.

"Transfer your Weight"

Whenever a class of pupils asks me at what stage in the swing the weight should be transferred from one leg to the other, I stand on one leg and hit the ball almost as far as I can with both feet on the ground. This proves in one simple demonstration that the golf ball reacts to the clubhead, not to a transfer of weight.

More often than not, conscious effort by the golfer to transfer his weight inhibits his application of the clubhead to the ball at speed, by encouraging him to swing himself instead of the golf club. That is why I so often recommend hitting balls with the feet together. Nothing more quickly gives the feel of using the clubhead, and prevents lunging with the body.

In the good golf swing made from a correct set-up, there is no need to think consciously about transferring weight. The good golfer's weight automatically transfers to the inside of his right foot going back and to his left side coming.

"Go Back Slowly"

This is nothing short of an invitation to disaster. It leads to **moving** rather than **swinging** the club back, in a motion completely lacking in rhythm. If you

go back at the pace that the slow-back proponents suggest, you have got to control the club every inch of the way, which, apart from anything else, is too much of a mental exercise.

What you should do instead is set the swing off **smoothly** at a pace that will enable you to come down quicker than you go up. I find most players swing at the correct pace when they remember they want their maximum speed at impact.

"Keep the Left Arm Straight"

Concentration on a straight left arm can often lead to no swing at all. In the effort to keep the arm straight, many golfers make it ramrod stiff, thus cutting down essential hand and wrist action. There can be no "swish" at the bottom of the swing if the arm muscles are tightened to this extent. Centrifugal force will keep the left arm as straight as it needs to be if you employ a true swinging action.

"Tuck in right elbow"

A right elbow flying away from the body is usually caused by a steep tilt of the shoulders in the backswing, rather than a combined turn-and-tilt. It is equally wrong, however, to suggest — as some teachers still do — placing a handkerchief between the right elbow and the body and keeping it there in the backswing and downswing. The right elbow will find its correct position if the shoulder turn and arm swing are correct.

"Follow-through"

Making a conscious effort to follow-through nicely when the rest of the swing is thoroughly bad leads to nothing but confusion and frustration. The initiation of the downswing completely commits you all the way to and **through** the follow-through. So, if you think your follow-through is bad, look for something wrong much earlier — possibly your grip, set-up, backswing or the way you start the downswing. Remember that a correct follow-through is the **result** of a correct start down.

What style of grip is best for you?

Should you hold the club with the overlapping or "Vardon" grip? With an interlocking grip, as used by Jack Nicklaus? With a two-handed grip, as used to great effect by Dai Rees throughout most of his career?

The **only** purpose of the golf grip, remember, is to square up the clubface at impact and transmit speed to the clubhead. If your grip obviously isn't doing that, then some experiment is essential. But never lose sight of what you are trying to achieve.

Finding a grip that will naturally produce a square, fast hit is a matter of intelligent adjustment. Start with the standard overlapping grip (little finger of right hand curled around forefinger of left hand). Move your hands to the right if you are slicing the ball, to the left if you are hooking it. Move them **fractionally**, a bit at a time, until the ball flight tells you that the club-face is square at impact.

If this doesn't work, try the interlocking grip (little finger of right hand entwined with forefinger of left hand), and go through the process again. If you have small hands, this grip might help you generate more clubhead speed, apart from squaring the clubface.

If neither of these grips do the trick, have a go at the 10-finger grip (all ten digits on the club). Be sure always that your hands face each other — the palms opposite each other — otherwise they will tend to work in opposition.

There is a correct grip for you. Finding it is a matter of intelligent adjustment. If you won't take the trouble to do so, accept the fact that you will have to make all kinds of compensations in your swing, through not hitting the ball naturally with a square clubface.

You don't HAVE to do it like Vardon

The majority of golfers find that the overlapping grip (top), popularized by Harry Vardon, best helps them deliver the clubface square to the swing path at speed. But if the Vardon grip doesn't seem to suit you, try the interlocking grip (center), or the two-handed style — both used by a number of great golfers down the years. These alternative styles seem particularly helpful to golfers with small hands or short fingers.

Should you swing 'flat' or 'upright'?

We hear a lot of talk these days about "flat" and "upright" swings, particularly with regard to which produces the best players. Rather like the "hands" vs. "body" method controversy, the plane of the swing has come to be a matter of much analysis and argument. The discussions are often impassioned, and mostly full of nonsense.

What is true is that there are two distinct mental concepts of the golf swing, rotary and straight line — to put it crudely, around yourself, or up, down and under yourself. All golfers fall into one of these categories; they think of or subconsciously "feel" the swing in one of these ways. And it is difficult to change this natural tendency in a player, even when it is so exaggerated as to produce serious swing faults.

I am fortunate as a teacher (but not as a player) in that I can swing either way — with either "shape" in mind. Consequently, I know that the rotary action (which is probably the more common) is very much a "plane feeling;" whereas the straight-line player, the up-and-down swinger, is not as conscious of his plane.

My personal preference is the straight-line picture, the upright swing. This is possibly due to my build (tall), and I would certainly not suggest that it will always produce better or more consistent results than a more rotary or flatter action. Physique is always the key factor in swing plane. Out of sheer physical necessity, the smaller golfer, usually standing well away from the ball, is more aware of swinging around himself (rotary) than the tall golfer who stands fairly close to the ball.

The big differences occur in body action. A rotary player must use a good deal of it, simply in order to get the club into a position from which he can deliver it to the ball, then to get out of his way while he does so. The upright or straight-line golfer doesn't need to turn his body so much. He can hit the ball much more with the swinging of his arms and hands.

It is possible to change from a rotary to a more "straight-line" swing, or vice versa, but I wouldn't attempt to get a pupil to do so unless his game was so bad as to need remaking. Even with a complete beginner, as soon as he moves the club I can tell his mental picture of the swing's "shape;" I know what is natural to him. I always hesitate to change this "picture," simply because it is so much easier for a player to operate efficiently with what he does naturally.

Thus, as in many aspects of the golf swing, it is wrong to be too dogmatic about plane — as some modern teachers try to be. Many first-class golfers move the club in and out of what would be the ideal plane, making automatic and unconscious adjustments during the swing. Nevertheless, I think it is true to say that, if you can stay close to the plane you established at address throughout the swing, the game must become simpler for you — certainly in the sense of your mental imagery.

Understand that the plane on which you can swing most effectively is much affected by your address posture. Think of your swing plane as an imaginary line from your left shoulder to the clubhead. If you swing your arms on this plane around a fixed axis (your head), your plane will remain fairly constant. In other words, your left arm and the clubshaft will come back to the ball at impact in much the same angle they were in at address. Obviously, this is an ideally simple mental picture of the swing's shape.

What is the *ideal* angle? Obviously it varies. A very short man who must stand a long way from the ball will naturally have a noticeably flat plane; a very tall man, who must stand close to the ball simply to reach it without crouching or hunching forward, will naturally have an upright plane. Your build and your posture at address will to a large degree determine your natural, and thus your ideal, swing plane. What is important

is that, once you've committed yourself to a basic plane by your address posture, you don't attempt to alter it with some artificial or independent movement during the actual swing.

Ideally, in order to promote distance and direction, the shoulders should be turned on a fairly flat plane. But — and it is important to note this — if the arms follow the shoulder turn too closely, if they swing on a similar plane, the entire swing will become too flat. This results in either too shallow an attack on the ball, very much from the inside; or a reciprocal flat swivel of the body into the downswing, throwing the club out across the target line. Ideally, the arms and club should be swung back and *up,* on a more upright plane than the shoulders turn on, so that at the top of the backswing the club shaft parallels the target line. This separation of shoulder and arm planes allows the body to move out of the way in the down-and-through-swing, while the more upright arm swing establishes a swing path from just inside the target line to straight through at impact, to inside again on the follow-through.

Since the arms *must* swing on a more upright plane than the shoulders, many people who believe they now swing too flat should not necessarily attempt to change the angle at which they turn their shoulders away from the ball. The only adjustment they need is greater consciousness of swinging the club *up* with the arms so that it points parallel to the target line at the top.

In an attempt to overcome a flat plane many golfers end up tilting the shoulders on much too vertical a plane. This leads to a steep downward attack on the ball. The body, because it did not clear on the backswing, gets in the way at impact, restricting the arms and therefore the hands and clubhead.

I believe the correct balance between shoulder pivot and arm movement is widely misunderstood, even by some of the top golfers. Certainly in the U.S., the move to a more upright swing, resulting from Jack Nicklaus's great success, has led to exaggerated body tilting — a powerless move for the average golfer, even if strong

young pros can get away with it.

If you feel some need to alter your plane — which means you will be trying to stop swinging your arms too flat or too upright in relation to your address position — here are two simple thoughts to work on:

TOO FLAT. Cause: bad address posture (leaning back); quick clockwise wrist roll backwards, accompanied by a swivel backwards of the whole body. Cure: Swing your arms **up** on the **inside** in the backswing, rather than around your body.

TOO UPRIGHT. Cause: bad address posture (leaning over ball); rolling the clubface counterclockwise into a closed position on the takeaway. Cure: Keep your head up, stand more erect, and swing the clubhead away in concert with the tilt and turn of your shoulders, but without any independent rolling of your hands.

Try 'two turns and a swish'

Golfers, I am afraid, like to make the game more complicated than it actually is. My simple definition of the golfing action is "Two turns combined with an arm and hand swing." And I am often accused of oversimplification when I use this phrase.

Well, here's a suggestion for you. If your game isn't what you would like it to be at the

moment, and especially if you feel confused and snarled up in theory, play your next three rounds strictly on the basis of "Two turns combined with an arm and hand swing."

Don't think of the backswing as a set of complicated and separate movements, but simply as the first turn. Think only of moving your right side out of the way as your hands and arms swing the club back and up. Simplify your downswing likewise. Forget all the stuff about head, hips, late-hitting, and what-have-you. Simply picture your downswing as the second turn — moving your left side out of the way as your arms and hands swing the club down and through the ball.

If you have a decent grip and set-up, and can keep your head reasonably still and your feet firmly on the ground in the backswing, approaching golf this way could do wonders for your score.

You will very quickly learn that the swing really isn't a complicated movement, and that the "secret" of golf lies in co-ordinating the turns with the actual swing of the club — not in a series of geometrically-exact, deliberate placements of the club in certain "positions."

Hip action–a critical shot-'shaper'

The action and alignment of the hips in the golf swing is a major factor in determining the "shape" of the shots you hit. I don't know how many average players realize that, once the grip and set-up are correct, the way in which the clubface is delivered to the ball — square, open or shut — is governed chiefly by the position of the hips through the hitting area.

Many golfers find this difficult to understand. Even good golfers, possessing more or less "grooved" actions in which everything works well most of the time, find it difficult to believe that their hip action may be responsible when they experience a bad patch. Yet such is often the case.

I can perhaps best explain the importance of the hips by examining what happens when they are in each of three positions in the hitting area. These positions are: closed, when a line drawn through the hips would be pointing right of target; square, when such a line would be pointing directly at the target; and open, when the line would point left of target.

If the hips remain closed as the arms and hands swing down, the right shoulder is forced to stay back, so that at impact a line through the shoulders would also point right of target. When this happens, in order for the clubhead to get to the ball at all, the right arm has to straighten prematurely. If this happens, and the left arm is not to collapse (bend at the elbow), the right hand is forced to roll over the left much sooner than it should, closing the clubface. Such rolling may take place before or at impact, and will produce anything from wild hooks to smothered tops.

If the hips are square at impact, usually the right shoulder will still be too far back, the right arm will tend to straighten too soon in the downswing, and the right hand will tend to roll over the left too early in the hitting area.

Obviously, if closed and square hips through impact tend to produce misdirected shots, the third position I mentioned — an open alignment of the hips — must be the correct one. That is the case — **with certain reservations.**

I believe it to be a physiological fact that a golf ball can only be properly struck with the hips opening — stomach turning towards the target — at impact unless the hands are used independently to attempt to direct the clubface in the impact zone (a sure way to inconsistency). Certainly, if one wishes to swing freely **through** the ball, it is essential that the left side be turning and clearing out of the way of the arms, hands and club in the impact zone. If it does not, the right arm cannot follow its correct function of straightening through the ball — it must straighten prematurely. Nor can the hands swing through and out to the target without twisting.

It is with regard to **how much** the hips are opened that we encounter the reservations, because the amount of opening affects the shoulder alignment, and the shoulder alignment is

the all-important impact factor.

To hit a golf ball powerfully and accurately, it is essential that the shoulders are roughly parallel to the line of flight at impact. I know certain deviations from this ideal are observable among tournament professionals, but these are compensated for by swing idiosyncracies that no one would want to copy. For anyone who doesn't plan to spend half his life on a practice ground, the more nearly the shoulders are square to the target line at impact, the better his game is likely to be.

We have seen earlier how the arms swing the club from a firm yet springy lower body base. We learned then that the swing does not originate in the feet and legs. Nor does it originate in the hips — there is no independent movement of the hips in any good golfer's backswing. The golf swing originates in the arm swing coordinated with the shoulder turn — **essentially a "top half" action.** The hips are in the lower half; thus in the backswing, like the feet and legs, they are followers, never leaders.

In the powerful golfer's backswing the hips are literally **dragged** into turning by the wind-up of the shoulders and the upswing of the arms. The hips resist this turn, resist without being rigid; in the good golfer's action they are normally

179

pulled through approximately a 45-degree turn as compared to the 90-degree turn of the shoulders.

When we come to the downswing, however, we require that the hips should be open, so that the right arm does not straighten prematurely, and that the arms may swing down and through, with the right hand remaining square to the line before and after impact without rolling or twisting. Thus, in the downswing the hips assume the role of leaders. To meet the conditions we have seen to be necessary for the upper body to operate effectively, they must have "cleared" before the clubhead meets the ball.

The secret of solid striking lies in the timing and co-ordination of this clearing or unwinding of the hips with the through-swing of the arms, hands and clubhead (see "Timing — or coordinating clubhead and Body Action." pg. 57). The balancing of these two factors is what the average player is searching for when he seeks "timing," and it is the factor the experts pray will hold up when the chips are down. Unfortunately for us all, however, it is one of the most difficult things not only to achieve, but to maintain. We tend to have it one day, to have lost it completely the next.

With the average player, the major difficulty arises through the effect consciously opening his hips has on his shoulder alignment. We have seen that, if his hips don't lead and "clear" before impact, the golfer will be blocked and out of position, and must rely on his hands to chop or flick the ball in the desired direction. But, when the poorer player **consciously** opens or unwinds his hips, he tends to overdo the action either by making too jerky a movement, or by moving his hips independently of the function of his arms, hands and clubhead. When this happens his shoulders, instead of being square through the impact zone, are opened too much. The result is an upper-body heave, or a collapsing left side, or an in-to-out swing path in which the clubhead never catches up with the hands.

Yet it is probably necessary to overdo both evils — not enough hips and too much — in seeking the happy medium. For those who wish to try, the following capsulizes what you are aiming for:

Coordinate the opening or clearing of your hips in the early part of the downswing with the down-and through-swing of your arms, to bring the clubhead to the ball with your shoulders square to the line of flight, thus ensuring that your swing path coincides with your target line at the moment of impact.

The less the clubface loft, the more sidespin will 'bend' your shots

The golf ball at impact with a straight-faced club does not slide up the clubface as much as it does when struck with a very lofted club. Thus less end-over-end spin (backspin) is imparted by the straight-faced clubs than by the lofted clubs. The less backspin the ball carries, the more quickly and violently it is affected by sidespin. Thus, even if you swing across the ball the same amount with a driver and a nine-iron, the driver shot will curve much more than will the nine-iron shot.

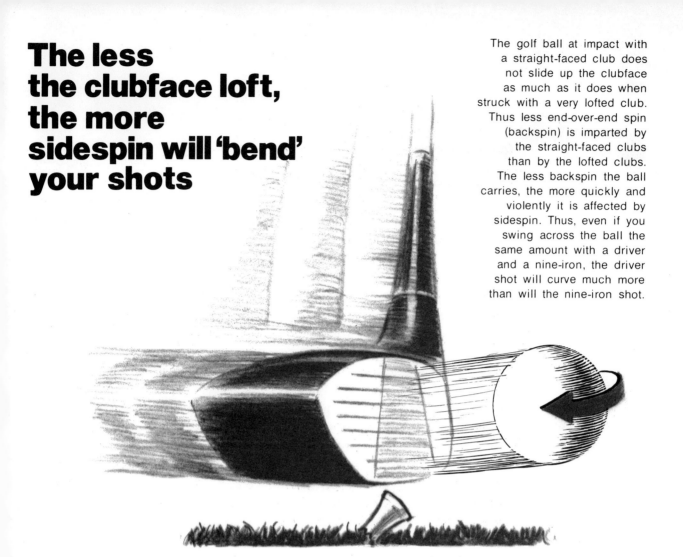

Why you slice with your driver but pull with your lofted clubs

Has it ever puzzled you why, when you are slicing badly with your driver, your medium- and short-iron shots still fly fairly straight?

When this happens most golfers assume there is something wrong with their driver swing that doesn't happen when they use an iron. I hate to disillusion them, but the fault is actually there all the time. The difference in flight arises out of the varying degrees of loft on the clubs themselves.

A driver is a very straight-faced club — it possesses only between nine and 13 degrees of loft. This means that it can make contact on only the very back-center of the ball. If the swing is steep, and across the target-line from the outside, and the clubface is open, the impact of the driver on the **back** of the ball is in the form of a pronounced side-swipe or "cutting" action. Consequently, a relatively small degree of force is used to drive the ball forward, and a great deal goes to create sidespin. Thus, the ball's weak forward impetus rapidly declines, the strong sidespin quickly takes over, and the ball slices.

Conversely, when there is a considerable degree of loft on the club, as with the medium- and short-irons, the "ballistics" of impact are different even though the swing characteristics are the same. Because of its greater loft, the face of the iron, although still open and cutting across the target-line, can contact the lower back area of the ball. This imparts more backspin to it. Some sidespin is created, but it does not dominate the ball's flight as it does with the driver, due to the greater forward thrust resulting from the backspin. Thus, with a lofted club, the shot continues pretty straight in the direction it started.

Obviously, therefore, the driver tells you most about your clubface angle at impact, and the nine-iron tells you most about the direction in which you're swinging. Use this information to analyze your game.

How my own swing 'feels'

I have sometimes thought, at the end of a long, hard day's coaching, how easy it must be to teach almost any subject other than golf. Mathematics, for instance, or carpentry, or anything — anything where you are dealing in facts, not "feel."

That two and two make four is easily demonstrable. But how

do you demonstrate to another being the feeling of knowing what the head of a golf club is doing; of "winding the spring" on the backswing; of co-ordinating hips and hands? As every golf teacher knows, the only way is by trial and error, using as tools demonstration and verbal definition, and working with them patiently until something "clicks." But it can be a difficult and exhausting business, and I am sure that a fortune awaits the man who comes along with a device capable of transmitting the "feel" of a true swing from one person to another.

It was with the fact that golf must be taught and learned by feel in mind that I was persuaded, some years back, to describe how I "feel" my own swing. The idea may be good, but there is one problem so far as I am concerned. Over the years I've had about as many different sensations of what I'm doing during the golf swing as I've had putters!

This, of course, will be true of the majority of tournament golfers, but it is emphasized in my case by the amount of study, and consequent experiment, I have devoted to the golf swing (to the detriment of my overall playing ability). I know for a fact that, in terms of "feel," I have swung the club in nine distinctly different ways while playing tournament golf!

However, there was a crystalization during that time, and I believe the swing I use today to be the one which is most natural for me. This doesn't mean to say that it won't change at all. In every player's swing, however grooved, there must be minor modifications from day to day to fit his moods, his metabolism and the conditions under which he is playing. And these, of course, are reflected by varying sensations of feel.

The overall feeling of my swing today is quite simply described.

I have the sensation that I am **swinging** — repeat, **swinging** — the club **up** in the backswing and **under** in the downswing, with my right side out of the way in the backswing and my left side out of the way in the downswing. Besides being the feeling I actually experience when playing golf, this is also the mental picture I try to cultivate when I am thinking about my swing.

In addition to this sensation of movement, I have another feeling which I strive to cultivate before, during and after the actual swing. This is a feeling of being "on line" to the target. At address, I want to feel that both the clubface and my body — especially my shoulders — are correctly aimed; clubface to target, shoulders parallel to the target line. Then, during the

183

swing, I have the feeling of trying to keep everything "on line." At the top of the backswing I feel that the club is actually parallel to the target line, and, at impact and for a short time during the follow-through that the clubhead is looking down and swinging along the line.

I might mention one other overall sensation that is important to me. Like most tournament golfers, I have felt the necessity to be able to hit the ball at various heights. This is vitally important in top-class golf (much more so than ability to move it from side to side). Thus, I have the feeling that if I uncock my wrists early in the downswing I will toss the ball high; that if I delay the uncocking of my wrists by an earlier unwind of the hips, I will drive the ball lower.

Now a look at various parts of the action.

GRIP: I feel that my grip is lighter than in the past, with a minimum of tension in my forearms. At one time I got "locked" in the wrists and arms, so that it was difficult to swing the club independent of my body action. Now I feel my grip is "softer" at the address position, enabling me to swing the club independent of my body if I so desire (this is not a recommendation, simply a feeling).

It is difficult for me to describe the actual feeling of the way I hold the club, because the grip is entirely natural to me — I was virtually born with a golf club in my hands. I have very little sensation in the hands or fingers when playing. Thinking about it, I would say that I feel the grip with the butt of the palm and last three fingers of my left hand, and with the middle two fingers of my right hand.

ARMS: I feel that my arms hang freely from my shoulders, both of them "easy" and fairly relaxed, with perhaps a shade more tension in the left than the right at address. I also like to feel that my "geometry" is correct — that my right elbow is closer to my side than is my left arm at address.

ADDRESS: The first thing I do in preparing to hit any shot is to aim the clubface at the target. I then take up my stance, left foot first, then right, and fiddle around until everything feels correct — glancing all the time at the club and the target to ensure that my clubface aim has not altered. My thoughts are chiefly on the clubface — pointing it correctly. The bodily feeling I am striving for might be described as one of confident comfort and "readiness."

When I've achieved this sensation, I have the feeling that my hands, arms and upper body — especially my shoulders — are "easy," fairly relaxed. But from the hips down to the feet there is quite a different sensation. In this region I have a feeling of tension — spring-like tension as though I were ready to leap six feet forward. Indeed, I feel as though the top half of my body, which is at rest, is secured to a bottom half prepared for violent action; I feel as if I am sitting on top of a spring-system.

When set up at the address, I have the feeling that I am "sitting" in such a way as to be able to swing the clubhead into the ball from immediately behind it — into the very back of the ball. The sensation in the lower half of my body is very similar to that which you would get if you began to sit on a high chair, but stopped almost as soon as you started.

I should add that I can see the **back** of the ball (and I try to look at the **back**, not at the top of the ball, as do many players), and that I have the feeling that my right side is "underneath." To be able to see the back of the ball is important. This is the bit I want to hit, and to see it and be conscious of it helps.

WEIGHT: I try to have the same amount of weight on both feet at address, and I want my weight on the flat of my feet, favoring neither my heels nor my toes. Just as poor players often tend to have too much weight on the right foot at address, good golfers sometimes get too much

on the left foot. I did this at one time and have to guard against it.

BACKSWING: The feeling I want at address before I begin to swing is that I am geared up to give the ball a really good cuff. I want a sensation of readiness and resiliency and good positioning that makes me confident I can pour the clubhead very fast into the back of the ball.

When I take the club away, the feeling I *don't* want is one of speed or hurry. If this is the case, either I am not confidently set-up to strike a solid blow, due to a fault in my address, or I am under-clubbing.

Thus, when playing well I have the feeling of taking the club away easily and smoothly, with no sense of urgency. I have the sensation of trying to keep the clubhead in an arc that is going to enable it to rebound accurately from the point of maximum coiling, where my shoulders are fully wound and my feet and legs are offering maximum resistance. I want that clubhead to really get moving, once I release the spring. Thus my backswing movement, above all, is a feeling of "drawing" the club back in such a way and along such a path that it will automatically rebound into the ball once I throw the switch.

TOP: From here on, feelings are difficult to ascertain,

185

because everything is so automatic and happening so fast. Sometimes at the top of the backswing I do have the sensation of collecting or gathering myself to deliver the blow — especially when my timing is good.

In fact, when playing well I have a very slight but discernible pause, during which I almost consciously "gather" myself to swish the club down and through the ball.

DOWNSWING: From here on in, my action takes care of itself. It is impossible, I believe, to make conscious or deliberate movements which will affect the down- and through-swings while they are actually taking place. Any downswing plans have to be laid before the swing commences, but they shouldn't

be necessary. The correct downswing is a reflex result of a correct set-up and backswing. Any deliberate adjustments at this point, other than an overall feeling of wanting to strike the ball firm and true, are likely to bring trouble.

Despite that, I do have one feeling through this phase of the swing which is the result of pre-thinking about the downswing: It is that my right arm is extending or lengthening into and through the ball. By working on this, I feel that I am hitting the ball to the target, not just bringing the club to the ball — swinging through it, not just hitting at it. The sensation is that the ball is started straight on target and that my extending right arm helps to keep it flying that way.

Getting more distance

All golfers want more distance from the tee. Many desperately need it. How do they get it?

First, they must understand that distance isn't simply club-head speed. It is clubhead speed **correctly applied.** If you want to know what that means, open the face of a seven-iron and swing as fast as possible into the ball across the target-line from out-to-in — play a deliberate "cut" shot. Now square the face and swing at half the speed into the back of the ball along the target line. You will

find that the second shot goes twice as far as the first.

Most club players don't lack distance with a driver because they can't generate speed, but because they fail to apply the very straight face of a driver squarely to the back of the ball. There are two solutions to this problem, which even the golfer with limited time and playing resources can adopt.

First, he can resolve to limit his efforts to create clubhead speed to manageable proportions — to the point where he has a good chance of applying the club squarely. It is because they have accepted the physical necessity of doing this that so many elderly golfers hit the ball so far relative to their strength. Second, the short hitter can dispense with a driver as such, and play his tee-shots either with a two-wood or a driver that has been given two-wood left. This is, in fact, for the occasional golfer, a way to "buy" more yardage, as well as better control, for the simple reason that the more loft on the club, the greater his margin for error.

Try it. You'll be delighted.

How to get the maximum fun from golf for the minimum effort

Every golfer I've met — including many a champion — plays the game with a fault. No matter how good a player becomes, he tends to err in some individual way. Even fellows like Sam Snead and Jack Nicklaus, whose golfing talent was Heaven-sent, have such problems: Snead has always tended to hook when swinging instinctively; Nicklaus crouches too much which makes him tilt his shoulders on too steep a plane.

We all suffer from some kind of built-in fault. Some of us fear a hook and some of us cannot permanently escape a slice. One man's hands tend to work the clubface shut, while another's will naturally return the blade in an open position. Some of us use our body too much, others not enough.

Many very good players spend a great deal of time and effort in trying to eradicate their natural flaws. They seek to build a swing that, mechanically, will always hit the ball solidly and straight. They try endlessly to overcome their individual faults. Some succeed, at least partially. Study and work bring them to a point where only extreme competitive pressure will upset the mental and muscular "groove" they have established.

The average golfer generally does not have the time, energy or interest to tackle golf like that. Nor is it necessary for him to do so to be able to play well enough really to enjoy the game.

What is necessary, however, if he wants the maximum fun for the minimum effort, is that he makes himself completely aware of his own natural swing errors; then, depending on their severity, either compensates for them or plays within them. In other words, if, like Bobby Locke, he is a born hooker, instead of trying to eradicate this right-to-left "bend," he can let it work for him as Locke did, compensating against it only when

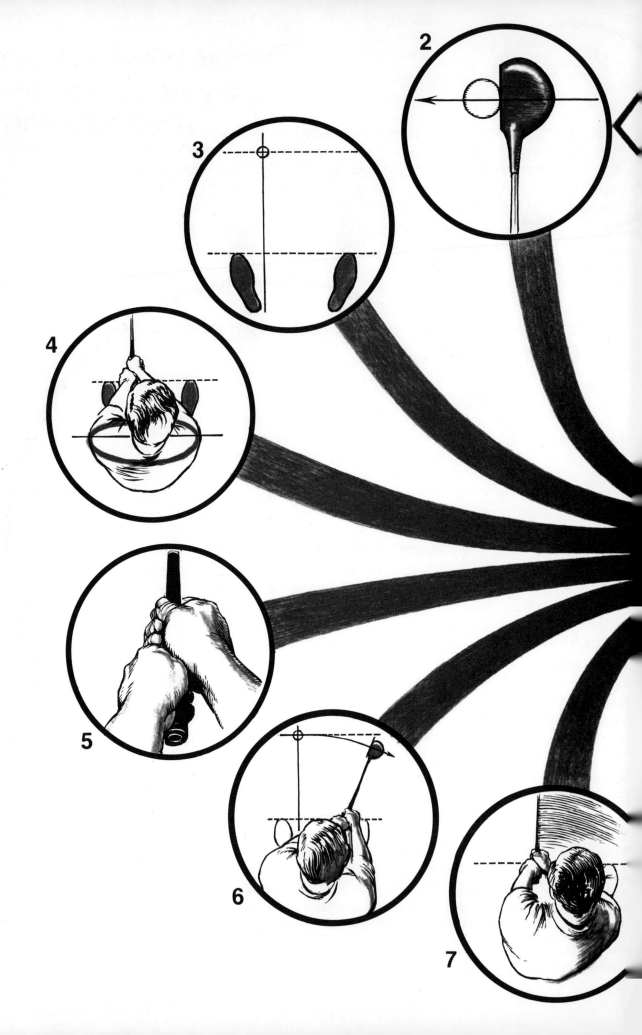

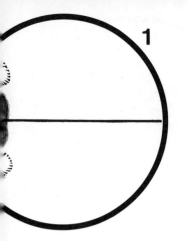

1

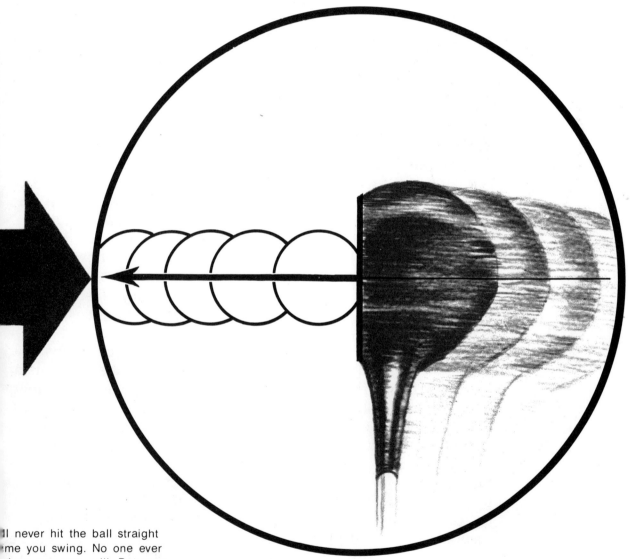

ll never hit the ball straight
me you swing. No one ever
d no one ever will. But your
s of getting close to that
ble goal definitely improve by
o achieve it. And to do that
st know and strive to apply the
al and swing factors that pro-
e perfect shot. Here they are:
aim the clubface squarely at
get. (2) With club aimed cor-
soles on the ground properly

and thus establishes the position of
the ball relative to your feet. (3) Correct
clubface aim and ball position enable
you to set-up with your feet, knees,
hips and shoulders parallel to your
target line. (4) Correct body alignment
and ball position promote a grip that
will naturally return the clubface square
to your swing path and target line. (5)

Correct grip and set-up promote swinging the club in the correct plane and
direction in the backswing. (6) Setting
the club in the correct plane and direction at the top of the swing enables
you — almost as a reflex action —
to swing it through the ball along
the target line with the clubface
looking in that same direction.

it becomes destructive. Or, if he naturally cuts the ball — as most golfers do — he can use his slice by allowing for it, seeking straighter shots only when the cut turns into a disastrous banana ball. The same applies to people who tend to hit the ball too high or low.

Golf's greatest plus is that players of widely different ability can enjoy the game together because of its unique handicapping system. If you can play pretty much to your handicap, whatever it may be, and really do get pleasure from playing and competing at that standard, then no one should hold it against you. The golfer who makes me mad is the chap who wants to play like Tony Jacklin after one lesson and no practice, and blames me if he doesn't.

By deliberately playing with your tendencies, rather than constantly fighting them, you will never become a great golfer. But you will quite easily reach a most enjoyable level of scoring proficiency. And you might be encouraged to know that most of the world's best players will usually be prepared to play really critical shots naturally; to let the thing fly in whatever is their natural "shape."

Making the most of what you've got requires, first, knowledge of why the ball reacts in a certain way — which I trust you will have gained from the earlier chapters of this book. Second, it requires the ability, based on that knowledge, to adjust your action sufficiently to maintain reasonable control over your more disastrous tendencies.

To end this book, I think I can help maximum-fun-for-minimum effort golfers by briefly re-stating simple cures for the main golfing errors.

SLICING is caused by a clubface open to the swing line arriving at the ball from outside the target line. The more the ball starts left and turns right, the more open is the clubface relative to the swing line and the more you are swinging across the target line. *To compensate,* ensure above all that you are not open-shouldered at address — aim your shoulders a little **right** of target. This will force you to play the ball farther back in your stance, so that you can hit it before the club cuts across the target line. Squaring or closing your shoulders will also encourage strengthening your grip — positioning your hands farther clockwise on the club which will help to stop your leaving the clubface open at impact. Most important, start the downswing with your *arms* to be sure you hit the ball before your shoulders have opened. The easiest way to do this is to feel that you are swinging your arms **down** on the inside path you have established with your shoulder alignment at address.

PULLING — hitting the ball straight left — is caused by the same shape swing as the slice, an out-to-in action, but the clubface this time is square or closed to the swing direction. *To compensate,* close your shoulders by positioning the ball more towards your right foot, and concentrate on swinging **up and down** with your arms on the inside arc established by your address position. Remember that the slice and pull are a pair, both produced by an out-to-in swing, with the alignment of the clubface determining the flight of the ball.

HOOKING is caused by hitting from inside the target line with a closed clubface. The clubhead moves ahead of the body and the wrists release "too early" because the body has not made way for the arms to swing past it. *To compensate,* position the ball farther forward and open your shoulders at address; this will automatically "weaken" your grip — position your hands more counterclockwise. Swing the club straight back from the ball, not "inside" or around yourself. From the top, start the downswing with a conscious unwind of your legs and hips, and ensure they keep clearing so that their action "leads" the clubhead through the ball.

PUSHING — hitting the ball straight right — is produced by the same swing path that causes a hook, except that the clubface is square to the direction of swing. Your arm swing is too much in-to-out because your body is in the way. *To compensate,* set up open, and clear your hips through the ball to allow for an inside-to-straight- through-to-inside swing, not an in-to-out swing.

HITTING TOO HIGH — if the strike is reasonably solid (i.e., not a ballooned shot) — usually results from over-use of the wrists. The "wristy" player who unleashes his wrists into the ball will always tend to knock the ball high. *To compensate,* bring the ball back nearer the right foot, shorten your backswing by cutting down on wrist action, and develop a feeling of swinging through the ball with your forearms while unwinding your hips.

HITTING TOO LOW — if the strike is solid — comes largely from a flat swing with too little wrist action. *To compensate,* move the ball nearer your left foot at address, swing **up** in the backswing and use plenty of hand and wrist action through the ball — "throw" the clubhead under the ball to toss it high into the air.

SHANKING originates from aligning "across" the target line with the shoulders "open" at address, which produces a twisting open of the clubface backwards in the backswing, and a flat, rolling action in the downswing that causes the clubhead to fly outwards. *To cure,* close your shoulders at address and swing the club up and down on the inside with your arms.

TOPPING has two main causes: (1) too much application of the shoulders in the downswing, which moves the head forward and thus narrows the swing arc; (2) hitting too "late." *Cure* (1) by keeping your head behind the ball on the through-swing, and (2) by using your arms and wrists earlier in the downswing to re-establish, at impact, the radius of swing you had at address.

SCLAFFING is usually caused by swinging too far back, the "rebound" from which gets the arms and hands working independently of the hips. Resist your shoulder turn in your legs, keep your hips firm in the backswing, then use them to "lead" the throughswing.

FLUBBING GREENSIDE BUNKER SHOTS: Open shoulders and clubface at address; swing easily into the sand on an out-to-in path; hit three inches behind the ball and follow-through.

SUDDEN SWING DISINTEGRATION: 1. Set club behind ball with face square to target and stand square to clubface. 2. Point the shaft at the target at the top of the backswing, and swing your arms **down** in the through-swing. 3. Lastly, my own favorite gimmick: think of winding up your shoulders and swinging your arms up in the backswing, and of unwinding your hips and swinging your arms down in the through-swing.

A final word of advice

The object of this book has been to help you to get more pleasure from the wonderful game of golf. Producing a book while still doing the practical job of teaching the game to individuals keeps me very aware of the limitations of written instruction. You can only play golf by "feel," and I hope in this book I have helped you to better "feel" what to do when you swing a golf club.

In all honesty, however, my final — and my best — advice is that you should seek out a golf professional in whom you can have trust and confidence, and who will have your interests at heart. There is no equal for the instruction, demonstration and explanation he can give to you as a unique individual with unique golfing characteristics.

If this book makes it just a little easier for you to follow such a teacher's advice, I shall be very happy.